To the congregations of Wildwood Baptist Church, Ashland, KY; Blake Road Baptist Church (Now Mesa Valley Church), Albuquerque, NM; Faith Baptist Church, and Dover Missionary Baptist Church, both of Scottsville, KY- Thank all of you for your love and support, and patience.

I also owe a special thank you to Dr. David Olford. He challenged a group of student preachers once to preach through the "Minor Prophets". I took the challenge. This is the second published book, arising from my studies/ preaching these oft neglected books of the Bible. My book, *Consider Your Ways: Messages from the Book of Haggai,* can be found here: https://www.amazon.com/Consider-Your-Ways-Messages-Haggai-ebook.

Most of all, I want to thank You, Lord, for rescuing me, and giving me a new life.

A Country Preacher Goes to Town
Messages from Amos
By Pastor Tom Leach

D1519051

Introduction

Amos, ah, Amos! If you had only known how eternally prophetic are your sermons. I originally wrote, and preached these chapters in 2014. I was struck then how closely Amos's context paralleled our modern world. I am even more awestruck now almost six years later. You will see, as you read this book, exactly what I mean.

Allow me to give you some general thoughts that will help you read this book.

1. I hold I high view of Scripture. God's Word is inerrant, infallible, complete, and sufficient. It is the Lord's revelation of himself to us. Therefore, I believe Amos was a real person, who preached to Israel during a time of great national rebellion against God.
2. The chapters were originally sermon manuscripts. As such, if it seems like I'm preaching...I was. Please be tolerant of any run-on sentences. Sometimes the spoken word doesn't translate well to the written word. There is a spiritual anointing, along with the voice's tone, volume, rate, and inflection that is present when preaching that is absent when writing.
3. You need to have a Bible open beside you as you read through this book. This is not a formal commentary, but I do "comment" verse-by-verse through Amos' prophecy. I use the English Standard Version of the Bible. However, any good translation you wish to use will be just fine.
4. I am a native Kentuckian. With the exclusion of seven years spent in New Mexico, I have lived in the Bluegrass State my entire life. With that said, when you read my prose, you may wish to do so with a "Southern accent".
5. I have tried to give credit, and footnote all references, and sources. If I missed one (or three), it was not intentional, and I beg the original author's forgiveness.
6. My prayer is that this work will lead you to seek a relationship with Jesus Christ if you don't already know Him. Also, I pray that if you are a Christian, that

this book will draw you closer to the One who saved you.

Pastor Tom Leach, Summer 2021

CONTENTS

CHAPTER 1: SUPERSCRIPTION AND PROCLAMATION 1. 1-2

One of the "defining" moments of my life occurred 39 years ago. I was 18 years old and a new freshman at the University of Kentucky. It was the first day of classes. Now understand, I grew up in a very small town. Not only was this my first time being away from home, but it was also my virgin experience with big city life. It would be a grand understatement to say that I was excited, and a bit nervous. As I walked along real, honest to goodness, concrete sidewalks, I thought to myself, "You made it out of Podunk; and are in the big leagues now".

As I walked along, I came alongside a large dumpster next to a small café. As I passed, I heard tremendous rustling and banging noises coming from inside the thing. Being curious, and naïve, I went over to see what was making so much racket. About that time, a wino roused himself out of the dumpster, looked at me and said, "Can I have fifty cents for a cup of coffee"? (It was 1983) Welcome to the sophistication of the big city, country boy.

Amos was a country boy. We'll see in a minute that he was a simple farmer and herdsman. He was from the little town of Tekoa. Tekoa was 12 miles southeast of Jerusalem carved into the rugged foothills.

Amos wasn't a professional prophet (nor the son of a prophet), but God sent him to the Northern Kingdom of Israel with a very strong prophetic message. Basically, God's word to Israel was this, "It's time to repent, or face My judgment".

If one were to take a look at ancient Israel during the time of Amos it would bear an uncanny resemblance to the United States of America today.

-The people had turned away from God and false worship abounded.

-There was terrible moral decay.

-The government was corrupt.

-The rich got richer by exploiting the poor.

-War and acts of terror were always a threat.

Though Amos delivered these messages in the 8th Century BC, they remain extremely relevant for us today. The eternal theme of the book of Amos transcends the centuries, and applies to us today. It is this:

It is time, actually it's high time, that people turned to God in deep repentance. If not, then they will most certainly face His judgment.

In this book, I want us to journey together, step by step, verse by verse, concept by concept, through this prophetic book. In this inaugural chapter, allow me to make some introductory comments.

Most scholars believe that Amos was the first of the "writing prophets". As such, he introduces his book with:

The Superscription. Verse 1

A "superscription" in prophetic literature serves as a sort of "title page". Amos' superscription is rather comprehensive. It identifies:

a. The genre.

He "saw". He literally "envisioned in visions". To envision or "see" translates the Hebrew word, *chazah*. It carries the idea of mental understanding as well as visual observation.

Reading through Amos you'll find he uses a wide range of poetical language, and vivid imagery. But don't misunderstand, Amos wasn't confused. God allowed him to understand what he saw. Amos then preached, and recorded, what he saw and understood. We have the benefit of reading his words today.

A lot of people don't see the need to study Old Testament prophecy. Since much of it has already been fulfilled, they can't understand how modern people benefit from these ancient visions.

However, even though a prophecy has been fulfilled doesn't mean it doesn't contain a universal message that is beneficial to all people, for all times. Amos' words ring true for a modern audience; just like it did for Amos' original hearers. God's Word works like that.

As we will see throughout the book, even the cultural context of Amos causes us to take notice. The parallels between the events in ancient Israel, and the USA today are too similar to ignore. Likewise, the counsel of Amos stands the test of time, "Seek Me (the Lord) that you may live!" (5.4a) God is ALWAYS ready, willing, and certainly able to forgive sin, and redeem a life, a church, and even a nation.

b. The author.

Amos was "among the sheepherders of Tekoa". He was a simple country farmer and rancher from the hill country of Judea. He was definitely a "duck out of water". God's call led him to leave his country home, and go to the big city. There, our simple farmer saw Israel's deep sin and corruption. He was appalled at the excesses, and blatant sin of the people.

Have you ever noticed that God specializes in taking the most unlikely people and placing then in the most unfamiliar and uncomfortable situations for His purposes and glory?

The late Billy Graham was once asked what he would say to God when he finally arrived in heaven. He replied, "Why me?" Why would God use a country boy from rural North Carolina to reach millions?

Why would he use such a simple preacher to advise presidents, kings, and other heads of state? Who knows? Why did God make Billy Graham the voice, and the face of modern Christianity? Only God knows. However, if you study the Bible, you will see that he uses the most unlikely people to do the most extraordinary things. From a shepherd boy who became a king, to a baby born in a stall who is the Messiah-God does the extraordinary with those that are quite ordinary.

c. The setting.

At the time of Amos' ministry, the king of Israel was a man named Jeroboam II. According to 2 Kings 14.23, "he did what was evil in the Lord's sight." Charles Fienberg describes the times in this manner,

Israel was at the height of her power under this king. The period was one of great wealth, luxury, arrogance, carnal security, oppression of the poor, moral decay, and formal worship. The moral declension and spiritual degradation of the people were appalling.[1]

One has to wonder if the current troubles in the United States are the results of our moral decline born out of our great prosperity?

When I originally preached this series in 2014, these were some of my thoughts:

- We thought it barbaric to spank our children. Look where that got us.
- We had an adulterous, lying president...the nation's response...well he is doing a good job. Look at us now.
- We started repealing laws that forbid homosexual conduct. We have not only legalized, but protected what God has declared abominable. Why? Apparently to express our modernity, and freedom.
- The states that have legalized marijuana for recreational purposes have really prospered. Haven't they? No, they are worse now than ever before.

Now, eight years later, things have only gotten worse. According to Scripture, they will only continue to worsen.

Isn't it strange that often the more prosperous and sophisticated a person, culture, or nation becomes, the more immoral and base they become. The true mark of the highly cultured, and sophisticated society is strong moral character born out of a personal relationship with Jesus Christ.

The superscription teaches us the importance of ancient prophecy in determining God's will and ways. Verse two provides us with the next thought. We'll call it:

The Proclamation. Verse 2

There is no mistaking the Lord's tone here. He is angry! He roars.

The Hebrew word translated "roar" describes the roar of a lion. It is a furious, ferocious, and terrifying shout!

Please, understand, God is kind, loving, gentle, patient, forgiving...yet, there comes a point when He gets angry. There is a point, when he gets fed up with His people living like pagans. It is at that point, the LORD roars!

Unfortunately, Israel had reached that point! God's "roar"

indicates He is about to pronounce judgment. This judgment will be in the form of the Assyrian army. We know from history that when the Assyrians invaded Israel, they just about wiped the nation off the face of the earth.

Amos also tells us that God "utters His voice". Literally translated this reads, God "gives His voice". It is an indication that He is preparing to intervene in human history. He is "fixin'" to pass judgment.

As Psalm 18.13 says, "The Lord also thundered in the heavens, and the Most High uttered His voice, hailstones and coals of fire."

You might take note here of the locations of God's "vocalizations". He roars from Zion, and He utters His voice from Jerusalem". This is significant.

It shows that the arrogant Israelites thought God was still with them, even though they were in complete rebellion against Him. After all, they were prosperous. They hadn't suffered yet, but it was "a comin'!

Sometimes God's judgment takes the form of disasters in the natural world. Things such as floods, earthquakes, and tornadoes, can sometimes be the result of God's righteous judgment. We know from this verse that two years after Amos' prophecy some type of major earthquake occurred.

Take note of the poetical language Amos uses to describe the vision. The grass has a personality, it has emotions. Things will be so bad that the grass (the shepherd's grounds) moans.

The summit of Carmel dries up or withers. The area around Mount Carmel was rich in in pastures, olive groves, and vineyards. Yet it will all dry up and wither away. It's bleak indeed. Remember God is warning the people, if they do not repent, if they don't clean up their acts and turn back to Him, this is what is coming. If they don't wake up, things are going to be bad!

I often wonder what it's going to take to get people to wake up today. Look at the obvious wake-up calls we are experiencing right now:

- Almost twenty years of non-stop war in the Middle East.
- The reality of our current economic situation. We are told it's good, good, good...but there are still children who go to bed hungry every night in our "unprecedented prosperity".
- The loss of two generations to the Lord. Only about 45 percent of people ages 18-35 profess any type of spiritual beliefs, let alone profess Christ.
- Disease and illness.
- "Natural" disasters.
- School shootings, and Mass Shootings. They happen so frequently they no longer shock us.
- The destruction of the family as we know it.
- Pandemic, runaway inflation, a government gone mad, the border crisis.

I'm not a prophet; or the son of a prophet, but anyone can see what is happening. It's time to get close to God. And, we better stay close to God!

Our God is an emotional God. He "feels" sorrow, joy, and anger. During Amos' time, God was furious with Israel and the surrounding nations because of their violence, idolatry, immorality, and injustice. As we look at our world today we can rightly assume that our God is angry.

The fact is- Whenever a person or nation rebels against God, judgment is imminent. However, God is just and always gives warnings in His Word, and through His prophets, so that people and nations will repent. God tells us in His Word, that when there is true repentance, He withholds His judgment.

In studying the Minor Prophets one finds a lot of gloom, doom and judgment. However, God is good. Therefore, we also find a word of hope as well.

We have the Word of Hope today. The good news is that though it may be too late for the world, (Just read the Bible; we know what is coming.) thanks be to God, it isn't too late for you as an individual. You are going to have to accept the fact the heyday of USA is over.

The "heyday" of the Pre-Tribulation church is over. The truth is the "heyday" of the planet is over. Anyone can see we are in the final days. Our only hope is to turn to our God in sorrowful repentance.

Jesus has promised to take the church out of this world before things get really ugly. There will be a time when "the Lord will descend from heaven with a shout". He will call up his people to be with Him in heaven.

We will live in bliss while God pours out his righteous fury on this fallen planet. The only way to join Christ in heaven, and "escape the wrath to come", is by placing your faith and trust in Him.

I was once called to our local Hospice Center to visit a lady that was very near death. I'm always a bit nervous in those situations. However, she was so at peace that I couldn't help but be infected with her serenity. I began to quote John 14. 1-6 to her. I started,

(Jesus said), "Let not your hearts be troubled. Believe in God; believe also in me. In my Father's house are many rooms. If it were not so, would I have told you...

At that point she interrupted me, and began to speak in a clear, and strong voice-"...that I go and prepare a place for you. And if I go and prepare a place for you, I will come again and will take you to myself, that where I am you may be also."

She finished the passage for me. She knew she was going to experience some pain. She knew that her life would soon end. Yet, she was full of hope. I preached her funeral a few days later.

I look forward to seeing her when my life's journey ends.

Look, you may not be dying, but you need hope and peace. Only Jesus can give it to you. In John 14.6, Jesus said,

"I am the way, and the truth, and the life. No one comes to the Father except through me."

Would you come to Him today?

CHAPTER TWO: GOD'S INDICTMENT AGAINST BRUTALITY 1. 3-5

Violence and brutality are very much a part of the human landscape. So much so, that I fear we are becoming quite numb to it. The terrorist attacks of September 11, 2001, were shocking, heartbreaking, and frightening. That day forever changed the world. But now, we have seen the images so often that we can sit there dispassionately and watch the Towers fall. We have viewed images of the wreckage in Pennsylvania, and the damage to the Pentagon, so long that we have become numb to the lives that were lost that day.

We have become immune to images of war. Fighting, brutality and violent acts on people just doesn't have much shock value anymore. A great deal of the entertainment industry glorifies the most graphic images of war and violence. It seems the bloodier the better.

Yet, we must never forget that God hates brutality.

Coming to the text, we find Amos, the country preacher who came to town. God called him to Israel for a brief prophetic ministry. He delivered the message that God was angry with Israel for many reasons. One of those reasons was the violence He found there. Many of the Israelites were cruel and abusive to their fellow countrymen.

God in His righteous and just anger is preparing to bring judgment against Israel. This judgment will be in the form of the Assyrian Army which forty years or so after the prophecy decimated Israel.

Before Amos declares God's indictments against Israel, he deals with the surrounding nations.

They were wicked and God was preparing to do a sweeping judgment that will leave no stone unturned. In this passage, Amos pronounces God's furious judgment against the nation of Aram (Syria), of which Damascus was the capital.

Now, the main burden of this chapter is this: God created man in His image. Human beings are blessed with a body, spirit, and soul that animals don't have. Therefore, it is particularly offensive to God when one human being brutalizes another.

Let's pull five main truths from this short passage. The first we'll label as:

The Lord Speaks. Verse 3a.

"Thus says the Lord". This is a very important thing to remember. This is God's pronouncement of judgment. He speaks, He has spoken.

The grammar suggests He has declared the judgment and it will not be revoked. The time for repentance has passed.

This is something that we need to remember. God speaks and His words are unchanging. We have God's Words written in Scripture. He has made declarations. He has made promises, and they are irrevocable. We cannot afford to disregard the Word of the Lord.

Truthfully, American pulpits need a whole lot more "thus saith the Lord". It just might start a revival! This is why all preachers need to be "Bible preachers"; if they aren't, then they aren't legit. We live in a time when the Lord needs to be allowed to speak.

I like to listen to other preachers. I listen to a lot of preachers, mostly on TV or on the "Interwebs". I have some favorites (John Macarthur, Chuck Swindoll, the late Stephen Olford, Alistair Begg), but every now and then I listen to someone I'm unfamiliar with. I do this just for a variety's sake. I am amazed at how many "preachers" preach without any reference, or at best, a casual reference to Scripture.

Let me tell you something. When I listen to someone preach, I DO NOT WANT TO HEAR THEIR OPINION. I DO NOT CARE HOW THEY "INTERPRET"THE BIBLE. I WANT TO HEAR WHAT GOD SAYS! THAT'S GOOD ENOUGH FOR ME!

The Lord speaks through the prophet. The prophet does not deliver a "personal rant", intelligent observation, or opinion. Therefore, Scripture is God's Word which carries divine authority.

God has the right to be judgmental, terse, abrupt, intolerant, close-minded, stubborn, jealous, strict, and dogmatic. (Thankfully, He is also kind, patient, forgiving and gracious.)

God has spoken, but what has He said? The next thought we glean from the text is,

God's Judgment is Complete. Verse 3b.

"For three trespasses, even four". This is a prophetic formula which signifies completion, or considering something in its entirety. God isn't punishing Syria for just one isolated act of brutality. He is going to punish them for their wanton pattern of sin.

Sin in ancient Syria was terrible. We know that they were brutal in their military campaigns. They also were very much pagans, engaged in all sorts of idol worship. At the time, Damascus, representing the entire nation of Aram, was one of the richest, most prosperous places on the planet. Damascus was known as the "Pearl of the East" because of its lushness, beauty and prosperity. But, God wasn't impressed at all. He is going to bring it all crashing down.

Think about the cities of Sodom and Gomorrah. They were representative of ten cities or a Decapolis. They were wicked. They committed heinous sin. Greed, violence and homosexuality were the rule of the day. God rained down fire and brimstone and completely annihilated them.

That's something to bear in mind. People without the Lord are going to face punishment for **all** their sin. God isn't going to let one thing pass.

Praise Him for His grace! If you don't know Him, it's time to face the facts.

The facts are that God's righteousness and justice demands that He punish unrepentant sinners according to the totality of their sin. He doesn't let you off for "minor infractions". The Bible says,

"The wages of sin is death." (Romans 3. 23)

On the other hand, God's gracious forgiveness through Christ is complete and covers all sin. The Bible also says,

"But the free gift of God is eternal life in Christ Jesus our Lord." (Romans 6.23)

The main sin of Damascus was its brutality. Especially its brutality against Israel. Next Amos tells us that:

God is Appalled by Brutality. 3c.

He speaks here of the particularly violent assault the Arameans made against Israel. The fulfilment of the prophecy is recorded in 2 Kings 13. 1-7:

In the twenty-third year of Joash the son of Ahaziah, king of Judah, Jehoahaz the son of Jehu began to reign over Israel in

Samaria, and he reigned seventeen years. He did what was evil in the sight of the Lord and followed the sins of Jeroboam the son of Nebat, which he made Israel to sin; he did not depart from them. And the anger of the Lord was kindled against Israel, and he gave them continually into the hand of Hazael king of Syria and into the hand of Ben-hadad the son of Hazael.

Then Jehoahaz sought the favor of the Lord, and the Lord listened to him, for he saw the oppression of Israel, how the king of Syria oppressed them. (Therefore the Lord gave Israel a savior, so that they escaped from the hand of the Syrians, and the people of Israel lived in their homes as formerly. Nevertheless, they did not depart from the sins of the house of Jeroboam, which he made Israel to sin, but walked in them; and the Asherah also remained in Samaria.) For there was not left to Jehoahaz an army of more than fifty horsemen and ten chariots and ten thousand footmen, for the king of Syria had destroyed them and made them like the dust at threshing.

Amos uses highly metaphoric language, but you cannot miss the message. The "threshing sledge" was an agricultural implement made of parallel boards fitted with sharp points of iron or stone. It was used to separate the wheat kernel from the chaff.

Have you ever seen a wheat thresher at work?

It tears up the head, rips out the grain and leaves a useless, wasted stalk lying on the ground. It is a dusty, violent undertaking. The metaphor implies very cruel, extremely violent, and inhumane acts. It's not much different today is it?

I was reading just this morning about some of the violence in Africa. In the Sudan, rebel soldiers, some of them just children, were taking infants and beheading them as an act of war!

They rape and mutilate women. They torture and kill the

elderly. This is exactly the type of brutality that sickens and angers God.

We do not get very far into the narrative of humanity until we find a terrible act of brutality. Cain and Abel were the sons of our first parents, Adam and Eve. Cain became jealous of Abel and crushed him with a stone. Ever since that day, man has been violent and brutal to his brother.

One of the things that America needs to take a close look at is our love of violence and brutality. You see it everywhere. You see brutal violence in:

- Movies... We have come a long way from the hilarious bar fights and bloodless shootings of black and white westerns. Now, depictions of graphic, brutal violence is considered "art".
- Music... there is a genre of music called "Death Metal". "Gangsta Rap" is all about killing, raping, and drug dealing.

I was going to give you some examples from these genres. But even country music has its share of brutal lyrics. Johnny Cash recorded a song called, *Delia's Gone*. Even the professing Christian, the "Man in Black", wasn't immune from glorifying violence. Read this verse from *Delia's Gone*:

> I went up to Memphis and I found Delia there
> Found her in her parlor and I tied her to a chair ...
> The first time I shot her, I shot her in the side ...
> It was hard to watch her suffer,
> but with the second shot she died ...

I wonder what God thought of that song?

Think about some of the sayings we use in everyday language. We say things like, "You really killed it that time". Or, "He really drilled that basket, goal, etc." We use violent terms such as "smoke it", and "whip it". I've even heard in church the terms, "kick some butt," or put a "whuppin' on it", or "crush it".

Oh God, forgive us our violence and brutality!

There are times when violence and war are justified. However, savage brutality, even in time of war, is especially offensive to the Lord. Extreme violence and savagery, torture, and callous disregard for human life breaks God's heart. He is justifiably angry with people, and nations that engage in such practices.

It is a Biblical truth that God places people in leadership positions as He sees fit. However, an evil leader that has no regard for God, or even common decency will not go unpunished. Which is the next point Amos makes.

Unrighteous Leaders (national, spiritual, etc.) Will Receive Harsher Judgment Due to Their Misuse of Power. Verse 4

Fire represents God's judgment. The House of Hazael and the citadels of Ben-Hadad are representative of ancient Syrian royal families.

In personalizing this judgment, we see that God holds leaders to a higher standard than their followers. Likewise, they will receive stricter judgment for their misuse of power. Amos is telling us that God is going to wipe out the entire royal families who have ordered the brutality and carnage in Israel.

This is a good time to interject a bonus teaching.

Remember that Israel is God's chosen nation. He has promised to bless the nations that support Israel, and to curse the nations that abuse or fail to support Israel. America needs to make sure we continue to support Israel and help protect her from her enemies. The truth is one of the reasons America has been blessed is because of our support of Israel.

One of the most wicked of all leaders in Scripture was an evil Queen named Jezebel. King Ahab of Israel married her. She then led him into idolatry and brutality and the nation followed suit.

Her "highlight" reel includes:

- The ruthless murder of a man named Naboth.
- Repeated attempts to murder the Prophet Elijah.

God eventually had enough, and both her son and husband were killed in battle. She met a very violent and gruesome end herself. God didn't have a sense of humor about her leading the nation astray. God has no tolerance for a leader who is brutal. He will eventually remove them.

God holds leaders accountable for their decisions and how they lead their followers. An organization, nation, even a church, over time will reflect the character of their leaders. A righteous leader will lead followers to God's blessings. On the other hand, an unrighteous leader will lead followers to experience God's judgment.

Amos gives us one final thought in this passage,

While Every Individual is Subject to Personal Judgment, when God Judges a Nation All Suffer. Verse 5

All ancient cities had thick, high gates that kept intruders out. The gates had a huge iron bar that locked them down. Amos says God will break (shatter) the bar of the gate of the city. This means the city will be overrun and the enemy will occupy the city. They will be cut off from their vineyards and fields. The leaders will be no exception. The inhabitants of the city will be carried off into exile and slavery.

Can you see what is happening here? The leaders orchestrated the war. They condoned the brutality of the military. Yet, the whole nation will suffer because of it!

We have a modern example of this in WWII Germany. How Germany suffered because of Hitler's demonic insanity. How many millions of German Jews suffered because of his orders? The major cities of Germany were bombed to heaps of rubble. Hundreds, if not thousands, of non-combatants died in the bombings and sieges. The nation was destroyed.

One survivor of the bombing of Dresden recalled,

It is not possible to describe! Explosion after explosion. It was beyond belief, worse than the blackest nightmare. So many people were horribly burnt and injured. It became more and more difficult to breathe. It was dark and all of us tried to leave this cellar with inconceivable panic. Dead and dying people were trampled upon, luggage was left or snatched up out of our hands by rescuers. The basket with our twins covered with wet cloths was snatched up out of my mother's hands and we were pushed upstairs by the people behind us. We saw the burning street, the falling ruins and the terrible firestorm. My mother covered us with wet blankets and coats she found in a water tub.

We saw terrible things: cremated adults shrunk to the size of small children, pieces of arms and legs, dead people, whole families burnt to death, burning people ran to and fro, burnt coaches filled with civilian refugees, dead rescuers and soldiers, many were calling and looking for their children and families, and fire everywhere, everywhere fire, and all the time the hot wind of the firestorm threw people back into the burning houses they were trying to escape from. I cannot forget these terrible details. I can never forget them.

Friends, let tell you, when God judges a nation, everyone suffers.

Even righteous persons living in an unrighteous nation, led by unrighteous leaders that condone brutality, and other sin will suffer along with the rest of the nation during periods of God's judgment.

Yes, God hates brutality. Let us all strive to live non-violent, peaceful, harmonious lives. The only way we can do that is with the help of the Lord Jesus Christ. We live in extremely violent times. Yet, God has called us to be gentle, humble, non-violent people.

The cruelty and brutality that Satan delights in extends to the most innocent and vulnerable members of society. If you Google "Myls King, you will find an image of a handsome, four-year-old, with brilliant eyes full of life, and joy. But, then you will have to read about his terrible death. I am including this CNN article in its entirety. Fair warning, it is graphic. However, it reminds us just how far humankind has fallen from God's glory. I also want to do my small part to honor this little boy, and keep his memory alive.

(CNN) — In the final weeks of his brief life, little Myls Dobson suffered unspeakable acts of neglect and violence.

A New York criminal complaint released Friday at the arraignment of Kryzie King, 27, with whom the 4-year-old had been staying since mid-December, said the boy had burn marks and abrasions on his head, neck, face and testicles. There were bruises and numerous marks made by an object on his abdomen and legs and wrists — bruises consistent with being restrained — lacerations to his fingers, abrasions to his armpit, and bruises and scars on his back. The child appeared malnourished, the complaint said.

Myls suffered "horrific injuries sustained over a period of days," New York Police Commissioner William Bratton told reporters.

King pleaded not guilty at her arraignment in Manhattan criminal court on charges of first-degree assault, first-degree reckless endangerment, endangering the welfare of a child and unlawful imprisonment. But Assistant District Attorney Nicole Blumberg told the court Friday that King also was being investigated on suspicion of murder, and likely faced additional charges upon the completion of the autopsy.

In a statement, King's attorney, Bryan Konoski, said: "My client is not charged with homicide at this time and she is presumed to be innocent of allegations against her. I would tell everyone not jump to any conclusions at this time."

Shortly before 11 a.m. on Wednesday, police responding to a 911 call found Myles locked in a bathroom at King's apartment at The Ritz Plaza, a luxury highrise in the Hell's Kitchen section of Manhattan. He appeared battered, was unconscious and unresponsive on the floor, authorities said.

The child was pronounced dead at St. Luke's Hospital at 1:52 p.m.

King told police that Myls' father dropped the child off for her to watch on December 17 and that she was the "child's primary and sole caretaker" until the time of his death, the complaint said. The father was arrested in December for alleged bank fraud, according to CNN affiliate WCBS.

At a news conference Friday, an adviser to the boy's mother, Ashlee Dobson, said that she lost custody of her son for financial reasons. The mother and the adviser, Tony Herbert, demanded answers from child welfare authorities.

"The city of New York put the child in the care of the father, who they knew was a felon," Herbert said. "You open up a case and then you close it thinking everything is fine? No. That has to be answered. Who did that, who authorized that?"

A call placed to the city Administration for Children's Services was not returned.

Dobson was in a shelter, they didn't think it best that she would be in that shelter with a baby, so they gave him to the father," Herbert said of child welfare authorities.

Dobson told reporters Friday that she was turning her life around in hopes of regaining custody of her son. She had weekly visitation rights but last saw her son in November.

In tears, Ashlee Dobson said, "I love my son. He always loved me. He always gave me kisses."

The complaint portrays the finals weeks of Myls' life as a living hell.

King told police that on December 29 she removed a hot rack from an oven with a glove and allegedly placed it against the boy's right leg, leaving linear burn marks, the complaint said. The next day, she told police, she allegedly struck him about his body five to six times with a belt, leaving bruises and scars.

The complaint said King admitted that from December 30 to January 4 she allegedly tied the boy's wrists and feet together with shoe laces and gagged him with a piece of cloth. She told police that resulted in scaring on his wrists and ankles. On the day she freed him, the complaint said, King allegedly beat him twelve to thirteen times with a belt.

On Tuesday, during subfreezing temperatures, King told police she allegedly locked the child, wearing only a T-shirt and shorts, outside on a balcony from 20 minutes to an hour, the complaint said. That same day, she allegedly locked the boy inside a dark bathroom for about three hours.

King told authorities that the boy was "being very difficult eating and that the last full meal he ate was on December 26, 2013; after that he would only pick at his food," the complaint said. The last time the boy ate or drank anything was on January 3.

Aside from her comments about the child not eating well, King gave no indication in the complaint of what might have prompted her purported actions.

Since arriving at King's home on December 17, the complaint said, Myls Dobson lost 20 to 25 pounds.

Julie Bolcer, a spokeswoman for the city medical examiner's office, said an autopsy was performed Thursday but the cause of death is pending further study.

By Ray Sanchez and Allie Malloy, CNN's Julia Talanova contributed to this report.[2

God, forgive us of our brutality!   Look, if you are a violent person please, turn to Jesus now for forgiveness. He will make you a new creation. He will help you overcome your brutal tendencies. He will make you a peace- loving, gentle soul.

Also, if you are a victim of brutality. God knows what you have been through. He is angry over it. He is a just God. Eventually, he will exact justice on those who victimized you if they refuse to repent.

But, you, you can turn to him for peace, comfort and restoration. I know, this is true. The Bible tells me so. I know my friend, because I have suffered brutality, and God brought me through it. I know, my friend, because I have been a violent, brutal person, and God has forgiven me, and made me a different person.

He will do the same for you.

CHAPTER THREE: THE JUDGMENT AGAINST GAZA 1. 6-8

One of the most intense scenes in the Bible occurs when King David was confronted by the Prophet Nathan. If you recall, this confrontation took place after David's adulterous affair with Bathsheba. When David learned that Bathsheba was pregnant with his child, he attempted to hide his sin. He called Bathsheba's husband, Uriah in from the battle front. David's plan was for Uriah to sleep with Bathsheba during his visit, and would think the child was his own son. However, Uriah was honorable (more honorable than David), and refused to sleep in his own bed while his men were engaged in battle. Therefore, David arranged for Uriah to be killed in battle. In essence, David orchestrated Uriah's murder.

David then put on the charade of a benevolent king, and married Bathsheba ,bringing her into his house. She then "bore him a son".

2 Kings chapter 11 ends with these words, "But the thing David had done displeased the LORD." (27b).

Let's pick up the narrative in chapter 12:

And the Lord sent Nathan to David. He came to him and said to him, "There were two men in a certain city, the one rich and the other poor. The rich man had very many flocks and herds, but the poor man had nothing but one little ewe lamb, which he had bought. And he brought it up, and it grew up with him and with his children.

It used to eat of his morsel and drink from his cup and lie in his arms, and it was like a daughter to him. Now there came a traveler to the rich man, and he was unwilling to take one of his own flock or herd to prepare for the guest who had come to him, but he took the poor man's lamb and prepared it for the man who had come to him." Then David's anger was greatly kindled against the man, and he said to Nathan, "As the Lord lives, the man who has done this deserves to die, and he shall restore the lamb fourfold, because he did this thing, and because he had no pity."

Nathan said to David, "You are the man!

Amos' prophecy in this chapter, is a similar situation. God, speaking through the prophet, is setting Israel up for a big, "You are the Nation!" moment.

God is getting ready to pronounce judgment. Concurrently, He will pronounce judgment on the surrounding nations.

In the last chapter we looked at the judgment against Syria. God would judge Syria because it had engaged in extremely violent war tactics against enemies; including the nation of Israel. Here, God pronounces judgment against Philistia. This is the land of the dreaded Philistines. God judges them because of their lust for conquest, and for engaging in slavery.

You can almost hear Israel cheering this particular prophecy. Remember, backslidden Israel still lived under the false assumption that they were untouchable. They believed that no matter what they did, God would never punish them.

At that time, ownership of the "Gaza Strip" was in dispute, just as it is now. National Israel believed that God would punish the Philistines, and they could claim Gaza for themselves. You see, Israel had become so used to their sin that they didn't even recognize it anymore. It won't be long before

God judges Israel for the same sin as that of their neighbors.

One of the main sins in Israel at the time was the practice of one Israelite enslaving another. What would happen was that one Israelite would get into debt, with another. The lender would then demand a large amount of interest be paid on the loan. God had commanded the Israelites to refrain from charging ANY interest on loans.

Inevitably, many Israeli borrowers were unable to pay their debts.

When the debtor couldn't pay, the lender would take the debtor, and usually his entire family as slaves. They would remain enslaved until the debt was paid. In many cases, the debt could never be paid, so the family remained in perpetual slavery.

There was also a great divide between the "haves" and the "have nots". The problem was the "haves" often exploited the "have nots" in their quest to have more. God was furious over this practice.

The Bible says that God created everyone equal. Colossians 3.28 reads, "There is neither Jew nor Greek, there is neither slave nor free, there is no male and female, for you are all one in Christ Jesus."

Slavery in any form, mistreating people that are indebted to you, bullying employees, or those "beneath you", are all practices God rather despises.

With this background, and context in mind, let's take a look at the prophecy against Gaza. We can look at this prophecy as if it were a courtroom drama. We enter the drama as the verdict is being pronounced.

The Verdict. Verse 6a.

"Thus says the LORD"- we must not forget that Amos is

merely the messenger. It is God Who has spoken.

The phrase, "For three transgressions, and for four" is a figure of speech that speaks of something in its entirety. It points toward the totality, or the sum of a thing.

In this case the "three, and four transgressions" speak of the sinful, despicable practices in Philistia; including their mistreatment of Israel.

We are going to key specifically on the Philistines' slave trading and violent conquests, but I found this fact rather interesting:

Philistine culture was almost fully integrated with that of Canaan and the Canaanites. The deities they worshipped were Baal, Astarte, and Dagon, whose names or variations thereof appear in the Canaanite pantheon as well.

The Philistines were also renowned for both their production and consumption of alcoholic beverages. Numerous finds have exposed a well-managed spirits industry, from breweries and wineries to retail outlets that advertised beer, wine, and strong drink. Among the most numerous artifacts unearthed from Philistine ruins are beer mugs and wine craters (large drinking bowls). The story of Samson's wedding feast alludes to the Philistine practice of engaging in week-long drinking parties, as the Hebrew word *mishkeh*, translated as "strong drink" in Judges 14:10, indicates a "drinking feast."[3]

By the time of Amos' prophecy, God was fed up with the Philistine's wickedness. He says,

"I will not revoke its punishment"-God's mind is made up, there is no changing it. For hundreds of years the Philistines had raided, plundered, and pillaged. Now, God was bringing it to an end.

The end would take place about 50 years later when the Babylonians fairly wiped them off the face of the earth. "Have you run into any (literal, not metaphorical) Philistines lately?"

Since they had conquered the five cities that comprised

their territory, they were probably feeling pretty invincible. Yet, God declares otherwise!

That's one of the things I fear for the United States. We have been a powerful nation for a long time. However, morally, and spiritually things are getting worse and worse.

Consider these headlines from the week of January 12, 2014:

2 children ages 1 and 2 were stabbed to death by their mother and aunt in an attempted "exorcism".

A medical examiner in Wisconsin was taking body parts from corpses without permission. Her reason, she needed training aids in order to train her cadaver dogs.

In Bristol, Indiana, two girls were gunned down while working in a grocery store for no apparent reason. We will never know why because the shooter wouldn't surrender, and the police were forced to kill him.

On Friday, of that week, there was yet another school shooting in Philadelphia.

On Wednesday of that week, in Roswell, New Mexico, a teenage boy shot two classmates in yet another school shooting.

Eight years later, things have only gotten worse!

Heaven help us if a school, or other public entity fails to provide for the religious, or social needs of every false religion, and immoral lifestyle imaginable. Yet, if a Christian wants to practice their faith, watch out, because that would be against the law!

At some point people need to wake up. How much longer is God going to put up with this foolishness? I promise you, it will not be forever.

God pronounced judgment on the Philistines who had a long history of cruelty, brutality, and conquest. They were particularly violent against Israel. God considers the totality of their sin, and finds them guilty. He then delivers an irreversible declaration of punishment against the nation.

God may allow an evil person or nation to continue for a very long time. However, there will come a day of reckoning when He has had enough. At that time, He will mete out His righteous judgment against them. All those who refuse God's grace should take note.

Now, God, through Amos, provides us with a prophetic flashback. Consider:

The Crime. Verse 6b.

"They deported an entire population to deliver it up to Edom." We don't know what this specific incident was, but it must have been well known in Amos' day. However, as we look at the key words we see exactly the nature of the crime:

They "deported"- this word conjures the image of sending someone into exile as a slave.

In ancient times (and not so ancient times) a conquered people were taken and sold as slaves. They were stripped naked and humiliated and sold on auction blocks. This was a sign of total victory for the conquering nation.

The Philistines did this to an "entire population"- the men, the women, the children, and even the infants were sold like trinkets. People, human beings, created in God's image, loved by the Creator, were sold like cattle. They were degraded and humiliated and treated horribly.

God hates this practice. Unfortunately, it still goes on today.

Take for example the story of a girl named Neary from Cambodia:

Neary grew up in rural Cambodia. Her parents died when she was a child, and, in an effort to give her a better life, her sister married her off when she was 17. Three months later they went to visit a fishing village. Her husband rented a room in what Neary thought was a guest house. But when she woke the next morning, her husband was gone. The owner of the house told her she had been sold by her husband for $300 and that she was actually in a brothel.

For five years, Neary was raped by five to seven men every day. In addition to brutal physical abuse, Neary was infected with HIV and contracted AIDS. The brothel threw her out when she became sick, and she eventually found her way to a local shelter. She died of HIV/AIDS at the age of 23

In one of the cities I served as a police officer a husband and wife team, owners of a fast food restaurant were arrested in connection with human trafficking allegations out of a fast food restaurant. It was reported that the couple brought people to the United States illegally, and then forced them to work in the chain restaurants they operated.

God help us that this abominable practice still goes on today!

Though slavery has existed for thousands of years, God did not institute it, nor does He approve of it.

He was particularly appalled by the Philistine practice of decimating entire cities, taking the inhabitants captive, and then selling them into slavery. God is still appalled today when He sees the epidemic of genocide and human trafficking so prevalent throughout the world.

It's estimated that between 21 and 30 million people live in slavery world-wide today. Even in the USA, the freest nation in the world; it is estimated that between 14,500 and 17,500 human beings are bought and sold each year. The average cost for a slave in the USA is approximately $90.

While most of us will never be involved in the slave trade, we must be careful not to take advantage of others that may be indebted to us; or that we have authority over.

God has found Gaza guilty; he has been specific about its

crime. Now, He reveals:

The Punishment. Verses 7-8

Fire is a symbol of God's judgment. The citadels, the fortresses, will be completely consumed. In other words, there will be nothing to protect Gaza from God's wrath.

Ashdod and Ashkelon were major cities in Philistia. In those cities, the inhabitants will be "cut off". The picture presented here is one of ruin and devastation. There will be no escaping God's punishment. Even the rulers, the kings and princes will not escape God's fury.

Notice the descriptive language Amos uses. God will "unleash", He will not be restrained. Gaza will feel the full brunt of His righteous anger. There will be terror. His hand will be against them.

Notice that the whole population, even the remnant, will perish. When the Babylonians conquered the cities of the Philistines they wiped them out completely. The image Amos describes here is of a few survivors being ruthlessly hunted down and slaughtered.

Zephaniah had a vision of this terrible day,

"For Gaza will be abandoned and Ashkelon a desolation; Ashdod will be driven out at noon and Ekron will be uprooted. Woe to the inhabitants of the sea coast, the nation of the Cherethites! The word of the Lord is against you, O Canaan, land of the Philistines; and I will destroy you so that there will be no inhabitant." Zephaniah 2. 4-5

God's righteous judgment against slave traders and violent oppressors will be severe and complete.

He will eventually judge nations who engage in these activities.

So what should you to do with this this section of the prophecy?

First, you should pray for justice for those who live in

slavery. Pray right now for those who are enslaved; even in the freest nation in history.

Secondly, you need to make sure you are not oppressing anybody in any way.

Third, you must turn to Christ. It is only through Him that you can be saved.

One of the nastiest, most ruthless slave traders that ever lived was a man named John Newton. Yet, he was miraculously converted to Christ, and became a pastor. Years after his salvation, perhaps in a moment of reflection on God's rescuing him from his wickedness, he wrote these familiar lines:

Amazing grace, how sweet the
sound, that saved a wretch like me.
I once was lost, but no am found.
T'was blind but now I see.

God's grace remains amazing to this very day. If you are lost, you can be found my friend.

[1] Ritenbaugh, Richard T. (November 2006). "Who Were the Philistines?". Charlotte, North Carolina: Church of the Great God. Retrieved 22 December 2011.

CHAPTER FOUR: THE JUDGMENT AGAINST TYRE 1. 9-10

Is it really all that important to study prophecy? Why do we need to go back into the Old Testament and dig out all these ancient pronouncements of doom? We know that the Lord Jesus ushered in a new era of grace. Most of the OT prophecies have been fulfilled, so why bother with them? Well, fundamentally it's because the WHOLE Bible is God's inspired Word, therefore, even the Old Testament prophecies show us some aspect of God's character He wants to reveal. There are general principles to be discerned in OT prophecies that can be applied to our lives today. Thus, the study and preaching of even a minor prophet such as Amos is very important to our development as disciples of Jesus Christ.

So far, in our study of Amos, we have looked at:

1. God's calling Amos from Tekoa to prophesy against the Northern Kingdom.

2. God is angry because of Israel's sin and violations of their covenant agreement- idolatry, social injustice, greed, and all kinds of immorality have separated them from God.

3. Israel was arrogant. They didn't think

God would judge them because of their special covenant relationship.

4. We also find God pronouncing judgment on the surrounding nations:

a. Damascus (Syria) - for extreme violence against their   enemies.

b. Gaza (the Philistines) because they had decimated an enemy and sold them into slavery.

What God is doing is tightening the noose around Israel's neck.   Through Amos He tells them of the nation's coming ruin. Israel thought they were untouchable, but very soon God is going to pronounce His judgment against them. They were involved in the very same sins as their neighbors.

In this passage we look at the judgment against Tyre.   Their slave trading and treachery had angered God and judgment was coming.

Though this prophecy was fulfilled thousands of years ago, it holds a contemporary message. Any nation that conquers and oppresses weaker nations will face God's anger. This also applies to individuals. God rather despises bullies. Bullies come in many shapes and sizes. Some are intellectual bullies. Some are physical bullies. Unfortunately, there are some spiritual bullies as well. We are also cautioned that Christians should take friendship, especially friendship with other Christians, very seriously.

Let's consider three main points, the first is:

The Ancient Accusation. Verse 9

Let me give you a very brief history of Tyre:

It was part of the Promised Land of Canaan.   At the time of Amos it was an island perched on the Mediterranean Sea. It had a very fine harbor and citadel that made it easy to defend. It is usually associated with its sister city-Sidon. It was commercial area. It was known for its exportation of a very expensive purple dye. It was the dye used to dye royal robes worn by monarchs.

They were also notorious slave traders. There is a large section of Homer's Odyssey devoted to describing Phoenician slave trading. They were also terrible pagans who worshipped a variety of Gods.

They were conquered by the Assyrians, and the Babylonians. Eventually Alexander the Great decimated the city.

I discovered an interesting note related to Alexander's conquest of Tyre.

The strength of Tyre was that it was an island. It was hard to reach. But Alexander used, wood, rock, dirt and debris to build an artificial isthmus to it. Over time sediment and other materials collected and today there are houses and stores built on it.

But let's return to the indictment. We find the prophetic formula back in use here. Three transgressions for four totals seven- the number of completion, or perfection. They are going to be punished for all their sin…their greed, their savagery, their treachery, their idolatry.

God declares, "I will not revoke its punishment." God has made up his mind, there is no turning back.

We need to bear in mind that individuals can always turn to God in repentance but sometimes it's too late for the nation as a whole. (Some people think the USA is under God's judgment. We are NOT! It may be coming. We see signs of it. But when God judges a nation it's bad…wide spread destruction, carnage, devastation, starvation… we are probably headed there, but we aren't there yet. Pray we turn back to God before it's too late!)

They had committed two acts that particularly angered God:

They took a whole population captive and sold them as

slaves to the nation of Edom.

The other act probably coincided with the first,

They broke their covenant of brotherhood. Amos doesn't tell us the specifics, but there are two instances where Israel and Tyre made pacts with one another:

In 1 Kings 5.12, The Lord gave wisdom to Solomon, just as He promised him; and there was peace between Hiram (King of Tyre), and the two of them made a covenant.

Also, in I Kings 9.13 Solomon gave Hiram the cities of Cabul because he had supplied materials to build Solomon's houses. Solomon referred to him as his brother.

In 1 Kings 16.31 we find that Ahab married Jezebel, the daughter of Ethbaal, then King of Sidon. This led to all sorts of problems for Israel.

At any rate, there was a long standing covenant of friendship and peace between the two nations. Apparently, Tyre broke this covenant at some point. The thrust of the indictment is that Tyre had acted treacherously, they had taken an entire nation into slavery and they had broken a covenant of brotherhood with another nation.

We see treaties broken all across the world today. Just look at the Middle East. Think about the USA's breaking the treaties with the Native Americans. Think about when a friend turns on you. These are all things God despises. One thing we as a nation better be careful of is our agreements with the nation of Israel. One of the reasons God has blessed us is that we have remained strong allies, friends with Israel, His chosen people.

Here again, we find God's hatred of slavery and cruelty in war. We also see that God rather despises the breaking of covenants. In context, He is particularly upset when peace treaties and pledges of loyalty between nations are violated.

God had tried Tyre and found them guilty as charged. Now He pronounces the punishment.

Look at,

The Punitive Action. Verse 10

In prophetic writing "fire" represents God's judgment. For example, He literally rained "fire" down on Sodom and Gomorrah. Hell is also pictured as a "lake of fire". To consume the citadels means that Tyre will be left defenseless. Its walls penetrated, and its sentry towers rendered useless.

Ezekiel rather graphically describes the fate of Tyre. We find this in Ezekiel chapter 26. I suggest that you take a moment and slowly read that chapter.

This did come to pass. What little was left of Tyre was destroyed later by Alexander the Great. Today, Tyre is a slum area.

God's judgment is comprehensive. He will totally annihilate Tyre for her sins against Him, and humanity. Nations and individuals who oppress others will eventually face His judgment. He will also "deal" with those who fail to honor their promises of friendship and loyalty.

Paul emphasizes this truth, while offering encouragement to victims of treachery:

Never take your own revenge, beloved, but leave room for the wrath of God, for it is written, "VENGEANCE IS MINE, I WILL Repay," says the Lord. Romans 12.19

We know what has happened to Tyre. We understand in context what is happening, and where the prophecy is headed.

But how do we apply these principles to modern Christian life? The text offers several implications:

1. Christians are to refrain from all forms of savagery. We are to respect human life and dignity and not "enslave" anyone in any way.

We are to voice our Christian views and practice them in

social arenas such as war and peace, abortion, marriage and the family, etc. Wherever there is injustice and persecution we need to bring the love of Christ.

Jesus says to Christians,

"You are the light of the world. A city situated on a hill cannot be hidden. No one lights a lamp and puts it under a basket, but rather on a lampstand, and it gives light for all who are in the house. In the same way, let your light shine before men, so that they may see your good works and give glory to your Father in heaven.

Matthew 5. 14-16

2. Hell is real, eternal, miserable and "appropriate" for those who fail to accept Christ by faith and repentance.

Jesus described hell as a place where the worm does not die and the fire is not quenched, as a fiery furnace, and a place void of the Spirit of God.

Jesus preached more about hell and money than He did about heaven. It a real place, judgment is real, the fire, worms, emptiness, pain- it's all real and you don't want to go there. You certainly don't want anyone else to go there.

3. Christians are to be "excellent" friends. Some things to consider then evaluating yourself as a friend, and those you call friends:

a. We are to practice hospitality.

Mark Twain quipped in *The Tragedy of Pudd 'n' Head Wilson*, "The holy passion of friendship is so sweet and steady and loyal and enduring in nature that it will last a whole lifetime, if not asked to lend money."

The Bible says, "Show hospitality to one another without grumbling". I Peter 4.9

b. We are to be "quick" to forgive when wronged. Also we are to seek forgiveness when we have wronged someone.

The Apostle Paul admoished the Colossian believers:

...bearing with one another and, if one has a complaint against another, forgiving each other, as the Lord has forgiven you, so you must also forgive."

Colossians 3.13

c. We are to refrain from gossiping about our friends (or anyone else for that matter).

'For lack of wood the fire goes out, and where there is no whisperer, quarreling ceases." Proverbs 26.20

d. We are to "stick close" to our friends in good AND bad times.

Think about the sick guy whose friends broke through a roof to get him to Jesus.

Think about the relationship between David and Johnathon.

e. We should correct friends when they fall into sin but always speak the truth in love.

"...but speaking the truth in love, we are to grow up in all aspects into Him who is the head, even Christ, from whom the whole body, being fitted and held together by what every joint supplies, according the proper working of each individual part, causes the growth of the body for the building up of itself in love."

Ephesians 4. 15-16

A real friend is the one who will tell you when you are messing up. A real friend is the one who tells you that you have something on your face. A real friend tells you that you didn't do your best. A real friend tells you that you need Jesus, lest you remain hopelessly lost.

f. You need to be careful in choosing your friends.

Paul wrote to the Corinthians who were having trouble choosing their friends, "Do not be deceived: "Bad company corrupts good morals." I Corinthians 15. 33

g. We need to be particularly loyal to our brothers and sisters in Christ.

In John 13. 34-35, Jesus said,

"A new commandment I give to you, that you love one another: just as I have loved you, you also are to love one another. By this all people will know that you are my disciples, if you have love for one another."

So, maybe you need to ask yourself,

What kind of friend am I?

A friend can make or break you.

Back in the 1950's there was a well-known radio host/comedian/song writer in Hollywood named Carl Stuart Hamblen who was noted for his drinking, womanizing, partying, etc. One of his bigger hits at the time was: *"I Won't Go Hunting with You Jake, but I'll go Chasing Women."*

One day, along came a young preacher holding a tent revival. Hamblen interviewed him on his radio show. Hamblen then showed up at one of the revival meetings.

Early in the service the preacher announced, "There is one man in this audience who is a big fake." There were probably others who thought the same thing, but Hamblen was convinced that he was the one the preacher was talking about (some would call that conviction) but he was having none of that.

Still the words continued to haunt him until a couple of nights later he and his wife showed the preacher's hotel door around 2 AM demanding that the preacher pray for them! But the preacher refused, saying, "This is between you and God and I'm not going to get in the middle of it." But he did invite them in and they talked until about 5 AM at which point Stuart and his wife dropped to their knees and with tears, cried out to God.

But that is not the end of the story. Stuart quit drinking, quit chasing women, and quit everything that was 'fun.'

Soon he began to lose favor with the Hollywood crowd.

He was ultimately fired by the radio station when he refused to accept a beer company as a sponsor.

He then turned to song writing full time and wrote "This Old House", written for his friend Rosemary Clooney.

One night at a Hollywood party, a longtime friend named John took him aside and said him, "What's this I hear, you got religion?"

Stuart answered simply, "Yes."

Then his friend asked, "You liked your booze so much, don't you ever miss it?" His answer was, "No."

John then said, "I don't understand how you could give it up so easily..." And Stuart's response was, "It's no big secret. All things are possible with God."

To this John said, "That's a catchy phrase. You should write a song about it." And as they say, "The rest is history." The song Carl Stuart Hamblen wrote was "It Is No Secret."

"It is no secret what God can do.

What He's done for others, He'll do for you.

With arms wide open, He'll welcome you.

It is no secret, what God can do...."

By the way... the friend was John Wayne. And the young preacher who refused to pray for Stuart Hamblen?

...That was Billy Graham.

You really never know the effect of your friendship and kindness. The covenant of friendship is so important. You should take it as a holy obligation.

CHAPTER FIVE: THE DANGER OF UNRESOLVED ANGER 1. 11-12

"Not forgiving is like drinking rat poison and waiting for the rat to die." (Anne Lamott, Traveling Mercies, Some Thoughts on Faith).

Lamott's proverb may sound dramatic, but it's very true. To have an unforgiving (or unforgetting) heart, to harbor grudges, to seek revenge, to "hold something against someone" will eat away at your soul until there is nothing much left.

This was the problem with Edom. This nation, who were descendants of Esau, held an ancient grudge against the nation of Israel which consisted of the descendants of Jacob. This grudge went back centuries to the time when these two men, twin sons of Isaac and Rebecca were young.

Jacob caught Esau at weak moment when he was hungry and conned him into giving up his birthright for a bowl of soup. Later, he deceived his blind and dying father into giving him Esau's blessing-his birthright. Therefore, the animosities between their descendants ran very deep. Over the years there were many skirmishes between Edom and Israel. The truth is they hated each other. The grudge was ancient, it ran deep. A truce to the feud had never been called.

And God was very angry about it!

The essential truth to glean from this passage is to "let go of the grudge"! We all have someone in our lives that have hurt us, who have misused us, or outright abused us. But we are to let the grudge go. Holding a grudge, harboring animosity, and possessing outright hatred is sin. It angers God, and will eventually consume you. Some people like holding grudges, it makes them feel good...yet...knowing how God feels about this ought to make us all want to give up the grudge!

The prophecy against Edom follows the same basic pattern as the prophecies we have studied in Amos. It begins with:

The Ancient Accusation. Verse 11

Amos follows the same basic pattern- Edom isn't being judged for one isolated incident or sin. We find in the archeological record that the Edomites were idol worshippers. We know from the Biblical record they were prideful and greedy. God is judging them for all their violent acts, for all their idolatry, for their terrible pride- for the totality of their sin.

God will not relent, this judgment has been pronounced and He will not turn back. Be reminded, God will always forgive an individual when he repents. But, many times it's too late for a nation, or an institution, or even a church.

The Lord now begins to spell out exactly how and why Edom has incurred this judgment:

The basic sin of Edom was their smoldering anger and vindictive grudge against Israel. This ancient grudge (which really was settled by the originators and picked back up by their descendants when they wouldn't let Israel cross through their territory during the Exodus) led Edom to commit a variety of sinful and violent acts:

1.   **They were constantly at war with their**

brothers.

In 586 BC the armies of Babylon came against Israel and destroyed Jerusalem. The people of Edom helped capture fleeing Israelites and turned them over to the Babylonians. They even took up residence in some Judean villages. This angered the Lord, for the Edomites, as descendants of Esau, were related to the Israelites and should have helped them. [1]

Look, man. When you hold a grudge the war never stops. It is constant. You have a tendency to look for opportunities to hurt the person with whom you are angry. You look for every little fault you can find and then exploit it to make them look bad. Now, Edom was extremely violent toward Israel.

To "pursue their brothers with a sword" means to always be the aggressor in war, even when the other person has given up.

A lot of times when hold a grudge, the other person doesn't want to argue or fight with you...but you insist...you pursue them until conflict is inevitable.

I've seen this over and over in families, on the job and even in church. I used to work for a guy during my law enforcement career who was a pretty good guy. He was very competent and was promoted to supervisor fairly early in his career. But, he was a bit paranoid. I think he had esteem issues. He certainly had a persecution complex. If anyone even asked him a question, he felt like it was a challenge to his authority. He would then start picking at the person. He would point put every little flaw in their work and even in their personal habits. He gave them the worst assignments. We tried to avoid him as much as possible, but if he was after you- look out-he would keep after you until he found something to hang you for.

Interestingly enough, he wound up the object of an even nastier person's wrath, which chilled him out quite a bit.

2. They had no capacity for compassion.

We know that Edom bought many slaves from the surrounding countries. They probably forced them to work in the rich copper and iron mines that were part of their kingdom.

Edom controlled this portion of the "King's Highway" which made passage through the mountains relatively easy. One Biblical incident shows their lack of compassion when they refused to let Israel pass through their territory, on the King's Highway" en route to the Promised Land. Take a minute and flip your Bible over to Numbers 20. (You do have your Bible next to you, right?) Now, read verses 14-21.

The Edomites' actions forced the Israelites to cross dangerous mountains, no doubt leading to the deaths of many.

Listen-When you hold a grudge, you tend to dial the compassion back. Someone holding a grudge is capable of extreme cruelty, even outright barbarism.

For example,

We read in the book of Acts where Paul carried a grudge against John Mark. During the first missionary journey, when the going got rough, John Mark turned back. His faith and dedication were not strong enough at that time to make a dangerous journey through bandit infested mountains. So he turned back. When it came time for the second journey, Paul refused to allow him to go. He just couldn't forgive him for backing out on the first trip. It was several years later, Mark had matured, yet Paul would have none of. Consequently, he and Barnabas had a bitter argument and we aren't sure they ever made up. We DO know that Paul forgave John Mark years later and longed for his company. But what could have been, had Paul dropped the grudge, we'll never know.

3. Their anger and desire for revenge "ate at them" constantly.

Edom's anger "tore at him perpetually"; their anger and hatred consumed them. This is a rather graphic description of holding a grudge and plotting revenge. It tears at your insides. Have you ever been really mad at someone? I mean mad enough to spit? It eats at your stomach doesn't it? It makes you restless doesn't it? It wakes you up at night doesn't it? It's not healthy or spiritually edifying is it?

An ancient Chinese proverb goes, "When you set out on the path of revenge you need to dig two graves: *One for your enemy and one for yourself*".

No wonder God despises grudge carrying!

4. Their anger spilled out on anyone who happened to be in their path.

"He kept his wrath forever". The Hebrew suggests an angry disposition or angry attitude toward everyone and everything. This tells us that Edom was a nation full of angry people. We would say today that they were "mad at the world" and nobody could have told you why.

Have you ever known anyone like this? There are people in this world who are just angry. Someone did something to them at some time in their life and they take their fury out on everyone around them:

1. The man who was wronged by a woman. Now, he hates all women.

2. The woman who was wronged by a man,. Now, she hates all men.

3. The person who was hurt by a school teacher, or police officer, or pastor...now all people in authority come under their wrath.

These are the most miserable people in the world. Unless they find the Lord, and give up that grudge they are destined for a miserable, lonely life.

So, we have seen the sins of Edom. Amos tells that God will not leave them unpunished. Next we find:

The Punitive Action. Verse 12

Here, as before, we find "fire" representing God's judgment. The Assyrian army would weaken Edom. The Nabateans would completely conquer them and assimilate them into their culture. God wiped Edom, as a nation, off the face of the earth.

The entire book of Obadiah is about God's punishment of Edom. He offers a very graphic description of what was coming. The entire book of Obadiah consists of 21 verses. Take a moment to read it and see if holding a grudge is worth it!

Make no mistake, God will eventually judge all hatefilled, violent "grudge-holders". For Edom, judgment came in the form of the Babylonian army, who decimated them. The message is pretty strong here. Any nation that bears a consuming grudge against another, to the point of pitiless violence, will eventually face God's judgment. Also, individuals who carry vicious grudges will face God's anger as well.

Even Malachi (the "tithing prophet") had a word from the Lord concerning Edom and its grudge:

..."but Esau I have hated. I have laid waste to his hill country and left his heritage to jackals of the desert. If Edom says, 'We are shattered but we will rebuild the ruins," the Lord of Hosts says, "They may build, but I will tear down, and they will be called "the wicked country', and the 'people with whom the Lord is angry forever."

Malachi 1. 3-4

So now we know what the prophecy against Edom was, and why God judged them. How do we apply this to our lives today? Let's think about some implications:

We must be very careful not to hold grudges, and be quick to forgive others.

There are a lot of ancient feuds between families,

between individuals, and unfortunately even between believers. The Bible has many things to say about harboring grudges, and the importance of love, and getting along with others. Read these ten passages. Let the Spirit soften your heart.

1.   'If anyone says, "I love God," and hates his brother, he is a liar; for he who does not love his brother whom he has seen cannot love God whom he has not seen." I John 4.20

2. There are six things that the Lord hates, seven that are an abomination to Him: haughty eyes, a lying tongue, and hands that shed innocent blood, a heart that devises wicked plans, feet that make haste to run to evil, a false witness who breathes out lies, and one who sows discord among brothers. Proverbs 6. 16-19

3. 'A soft answer turns away wrath, but a harsh word stirs up anger". Proverbs 15.1

4. "A fool gives full vent to his spirit, but a wise man quietly holds it back." Proverbs 29.11

5. 'A hot-tempered man stirs up strife, but he who is slow to anger quiets contention." Proverbs 15.18

6. 'You shall not take vengeance or bear a grudge against the sons of your own people, but you shall love your neighbor as yourself: I am the Lord."

Leviticus 19.18

7. "And whenever you stand praying, forgive, if you have anything against anyone, so that your Father also who is in heaven may forgive you your trespasses."

Mark 11.25

8. "Hatred stirs up strife, but love covers all offenses." Proverbs 10.12

9. 'Let all bitterness and wrath and anger and clamor and slander be put away from you, along with all malice." Ephesians 4.31

10. For we ourselves were once foolish, disobedient, led astray, slaves to various passions and pleasures, passing our days in malice and envy, hated by others and hating one another. But when the goodness and loving kindness of God our Savior appeared, He saved us..." Titus 3. 3-5a

I pray you see that the Bible is crystal clear that unresolved anger is a dangerous spiritual place to be.

Webster's dictionary defines "grudge" like this-"a strong continued feeling of hostility or ill will against someone over a real or fancied grievance."

Everywhere you look today you see grudges, many of them resulting in violence. Nations hold grudges against other nations. Wars are started, people die, people suffer, and things are destroyed.

Grudges are held in marriages.

Grudges between children and parents.

Grudges are held between co-workers.

Grudges between students.

And the worse kind of grudges, and the last place on earth you want grudges to be held is in the church. But it's becoming more and more the reality today. I've lost count now of how many people have completely left the church over unresolved anger and ungodly grudges. I have lived to see grudges not only destroy churches, but lives as well. I could probably take you to ten homes right now where people aren't going to church anywhere because they are holding grudges against fellow Christians.

O, church, isn't it time you gave up the grudge? Isn't it time you made up with whoever you are angry with?

Jesus said if you go to pray and have a grudge against someone, you are to quit praying, go make up, then come back and pray.

Isn't part of the Lord's Prayer, "forgive us our trespasses as we forgive those who trespass against us"?

I can tell you from personal experience…holding anger will mess you up! It will break your fellowship with God. It will ruin your health. It will ruin all your relationships. Don't suffer the fate of Edom…give up the grudge!

[1] Preface to Obadiah in ESV: 1200

[2] Passages from the Holy Bible English Standard Version

CHAPTER SIX: THE NOOSE TIGHTENS: 1. 13-2.5

Have you ever played the game "Hide the Thimble"? It's the children's game where you have a group of people gathered in a room. One person is selected to be "it". This person leaves the room. Then a thimble or other small object is hidden in the room. The "it" person comes in and starts to look around the room for the thimble. If the person is far away from the object everybody yells "cold". If they start getting closer to the object they yell "warm!" The closer they get you yet the group yells, "Warmer", then warmer!" They get closer, hot, hot HOT, HOTTER, smoking"...until the object is found. I heard about a version of this game where instead of yelling, cold, warm, warmer or HOT, the people sang a song. The closer the person got to the object the louder the group sings...that actually sounds like fun.

The Jews in the Northern kingdom must have been wondering what Amos was getting at as he pronounced judgment on the surrounding nations.

They had become so calloused in their sin and rebellion against God that they didn't realize the prophecy was closing in on them- the true object of God's anger. They thought Amos was pretty cold in regard to their behavior when in fact he was getting hotter and hotter, closer and closer, to pronouncing

God's judgment against them.

This passage examines the judgments against the final three nations before God turns His attention directly toward Israel.

Amos' prophecies in this section of the book read almost like today's newspapers. Though times have changed, and culture has changed, God hasn't changed! There are certain things that He hates, there are sins He will judge unless people turn to Christ in faith and repentance.

There is a message for the country and the church in these verses. The world is falling apart around us. Nigeria, the Ukraine, China, all of Europe, Australia, Greece, Iceland...no place on earth right now isn't in turmoil of some kind. God may very well be playing "hide the thimble with the USA". It is getting hotter and that's just the truth.

Let's see what we can learn from God's judgment of these three nations. Let's look first at,

Ammon: God's Anger Over Wartime Atrocities.

Verses 13-15

Amos follows the familiar pattern. He will deliver God's indictment, and then pronounce His punishment.

The first two nations mentioned in the passage Ammon and Moab bordered Israel. The history of these nations is rather sordid. They originated when right after Lot and his daughters escaped Sodom and Gomorrah. They fled into the hill country of Zoar and hid out in a cave. The two daughters thought that everyone on the world had been destroyed but them. They panicked. They mistakenly thought they would have to repopulate the world. So they got their father, Lot drunk and seduced him. They each had one male child, one Ammon and the other Moab. You can read this for yourself in Genesis 19.30-38.

During the Exodus, the Ammonites and Israelites developed hostilities resulting in skirmishes that continued through the time of the prophets. You can read about this in Deuteronomy 2 and 23, Judges 10-11, and I Samuel 11.

Now that you have the background, let's look at the particular issue with Ammon. First, consider

The Indictment. Verse 13

Once again Gilead is the object of foreign aggression. Remember Damascus had been particularly brutal to the region of Gilead. Gilead was a very lush area in the desert region just north of Israel. It was mountainous and well watered by the Jordan River. It was known for its grapes, fruit trees, and pasture lands. It was also well timbered.

It was where the "balm of Gilead" an ancient medicine was made. The Ammonites wanted the rich resources found in Gilead.

The Ammonites had committed unspeakable acts of violence during a time of war. They had slaughtered innocent non-combatants that posed no threats to their soldiers. This is a particularly graphic scene of violence. The Scriptures don't record a particular incident where women and the unborn were treated so brutally. Amos could have been speaking metaphorically of the killing of non-combatants. He could have also been speaking of something that was common knowledge... we really don't know and it's best not to speculate.

We do see the driving force behind Ammon's extreme violence...GREED. They wanted to "enlarge their borders". They wanted more territory for themselves. They wanted the rich land of Gilead and they would stop at nothing to get it.

Now, look at:

The Punishment. Verses 14-15

We see God's judgment depicted as fire, as a wind, as shouting, as a "tempest in the day of the whirlwind".

A tempest is a "violent storm with high winds, esp. one accompanied by rain, hail or snow". The tempest would come in the form of the Assyrian army that would invade Ammon and violently assault them.

They would deport their rulers and replace them with a puppet government.

Eventually the entire race will be exterminated. They no longer exist.

There have been similar atrocities in modern times Hitler's wartime atrocities are an example of the type of brutality God hates. The Mai Lai incident during the Viet Nam war is an example of Americans engaging in this sort of violence... The 911 attacks are another example.

The Boston Marathon bomb killed three and injured 264 others.

Just yesterday a group of terrorists armed with "long knives" attacked innocent men, women and children in a railway station in SW China. According to Chinese State Newspaper 29 people were killed and 133 were seriously wounded. Last month 21 people including women and children were killed by a suicide bomber while eating at a restaurant in Kabul, Afghanistan.

It never ends!

So what do we do with this historical truth?

The Application.

Scripture does teach that there is a "time for war" (Ecclesiastes 3.8). However, extreme brutality, especially against the "civilian population", is an affront to God.

In a broader context we must be careful not to hurt the

"innocents" around us in our daily battles. There is also a reminder here of God's love of the unborn.

Amos gets a little "hotter" as he moves closer to Israel. Next, jump over to chapter two, where we find the judgment against,

Moab: God's Anger Over Idolatry and Inhumanity.

Here again, we begin with:

The Indictment. Verse 1

Don't miss the indictment formula Amos once again uses here. "For three transgressions, and for four", for all their sin, not just an isolated incident ,God is going to punish Moab.

His punishment is sure...it is irrevocable...He has declared it and there is no turning back.

The Moabites were known for their idolatry and use of religious prostitutes. They were also known as a very warlike people that exercised extreme brutality towards their enemies. We do know that Moab and Israel were sworn enemies and were often at war with one another.

Here again, Amos describes an incident that isn't recorded in Scripture yet must have been a well know event at the time of the prophecy.

One Jewish tradition holds that the king of Moab killed the king of Edom. Then he burned his bones down to lime and painted the walls of his palace with them.

Moab's desecration of the King of Moab's corpse shows a lack of regard for basic human dignity and an insatiable blood lust. The Moabite's practice of idolatry, even to the point of human sacrifice, had numbed their hearts to all that was holy.

Now, look at,

The Punishment. Verses 2-3

There will be no defense for Moab; they will die in a violent, military campaign. God is a God of justice and He allowed Moab to suffer as they had caused others to suffer.

The Bible says to be careful because you will "reap what you sow". (Galatians 6. 7-9) Once again we find God using conquering invaders to decimate the nation and eradicate this entire population. The entire race was exterminated because of their sin.

"Ok", you might say, "but what does this have to do with me, or the modern world?" Think about the application:

Extreme idolatry, immorality and violence can harden your heart to the point that you no longer have respect for anything. This unholy trinity can also cause you to lose all reservation and control over your actions.

I used this illustration years ago when I first preached this series. Now, (Feburary, 2022) look at the events in Ukraine.

We see this all over the world right now. In Ukraine the death toll is up to 100 or more.

With Russia deploying troops, get ready for more bloodshed if not all out war involving several nations- including the USA.

In 2012, the demonic possessed James Egan Holmes went into the Century Movie Theater in Aurora, CO and shot and killed 12 people. 70 others were shot, but survived their wounds.

There are many reasons acts of violence don't seem to faze us anymore, but they really should. Amos has gone from hot, to hotter, now he gets even hotter as he prophesies against the southern kingdom-Judah.

God's Anger Over Willful Sin. Verses 4-5

The opening part of verse 4 follows the same indictment formula. The punishment is irrevocable. The second half of verse 4 provides the details of the "two-count" indictment.

The Indictment.

1. Judah had totally rejected the Lord's Law and His directives. They had entered into a state of total rebellion where their actions were in total opposition to what God demanded of them.

They followed after lies (false gods and false prophets) they were full of greed, and violence and inhumanity.

2. Judah had fallen into severe idolatry and was totally corrupt.

And the punishment?

Judah would experience war, occupation and exile from the Promised Land. The Babylonian captivity would soon commence. Jerusalem, the city of peace would lie in ruins.

Doesn't the message in this section prick our consciences?

Christians (and nations under God) must be very careful to avoid idolatry in any form. God is a jealous God and demands to be the sole object of our worship. We are constantly bombarded with lies. The world the flesh and the devil all conspire to lead us down the path of destruction. We must stay close to God and make Him our number one priority.

We must be extremely cautious as God's people to avoid being seduced and lead astray by the enemy's lies. And they can be quite seducing, even entertaining.

AW Tozer offers some warnings that Dr. Al Mohler quotes in his book: *He is Not Silent" Preaching in a Post-Modern World:*

We have the breezy, self-confident Christians with little affinity for Christ and his cross. We have the joy-bell boys that can bounce out there and look as much like a game show host as possible. Yet, they are Jesus' sake?! The hypocrites!

They are not doing it for Jesus' sake at all; they are doing it in their own carnal flesh and are using the church as a theater because they haven't yet reached the place where the legitimate theater would take them.

Tozer takes his arguement further,

It is now common practice in most evangelical churches to offer the people, especially the young people, a maximum of entertainment and a minimum of serious instruction. It is scarcely possible in most places to get anyone to attend meetings where the only attraction is God. One can only conclude that God's professed children are bored with him, for they must be wooed to meeting with a stick of striped candy in the form of religious movies, games, and refreshments

This has influenced the whole pattern of church life, and even brought into being a new type of church architecture designed to house the golden calf.

So we have this strange anomaly of orthodoxy in creed and heterodoxy in practice. The striped-candy technique has been so fully integrated ino our present religious thinking that it is simply taken for granted. Its victims never dream that it is not part of the teachings of Christ and His apostles.

Any objection to the carryings-on of our present goldencalf Christianity is met with the triumphant reply, "But we are winning them!" And winning them to what? To true discipleship? To cross carrying? To self-denial? To separation from the world? To crucifixion of the flesh? To holy living? To nobility of character? To a despising of the the world's treasures?

To hard self-discipline?   To love for God?   To total commital to Christ? Of course, to all these questions is "no".

So, we must ask ourselves, "Where does this passage lead us?" It should lead us to the foot of the cross of Jesus Christ.

We live in a time of unprecedented violence and war and inhumanity.

We watch the grossest forms murders and assault on primetime TV and call it GOOD, ENTERTAINING DRAMA... GOD HELP US!

We can go to sleep at night without praying for God to sweep this world with a revival and spiritual awakening. We play church and denominational politics when people are eternally lost and going to hell. There's only one place to go...to Jesus Christ, our only Hope and our only peace...

Would you join me at the cross?

CHAPTER 7:
GOD'S HATRED
OF INJUSTICE,
IMMORALITY AND
IRREVERENCE 2. 6-16

It doesn't take a very astute observer to see that society in general is marked by social injustice, immorality and irreverence.

You know and I know that in this economy, the poor get poorer and the rich get richer.

Years ago, I was asked to assist a family with the purchase of some medicine for two children. When I went to the pharmacy to make the purchase, I was told the medicine would cost two-hundred dollars. That seemed like a lot of money to me, so I asked the name and purpose of it.

I was a bit shocked when the pharmacist told me it was a very common, and inexpensive over-the-counter laxative. I checked the price of the very same medicine, on the shelf in the very same pharmacy. It cost just $1.99! I asked the pharmacist if she offered the two dollar medicine to this poor family. She just shrugged her shoulders!

Our nation now "recognizes" same sex marriages. Homosexual couples now have the same rights and privileges of heterosexual couples.

And irreverence? I think I can make the point and show you how far things have gone in the direction of irreverence by telling you the title of a sermon series by the pastor of a church in Eugene Oregon: "Church Sucks", that's the name of the series.

Is this really the depths the church has sank in the atttempt to appeal to the post-Christian culture? Let me teach you a Greek expression often used by the Apostle Paul when he was blown away by something, *me genito*- God forbid!

The introductory sections of Amos have come to a close... the warm up is over. Israel has been primed. The noose has been tightened. God has their attention. Now, God speaking through Amos gets to the point. This judgment is about Israel and their sin. His indictments will continue through the remainder of the book.

In looking at this passage we see that God has a tender spot for the poor. He commands His people to be tender toward them as well. God also calls His people to a high standard of morality, especially sexual morality.

We also see that worship should be reverent, holy and God-centered.

If you had to hang your thoughts on one main teaching in this passage it would be this: **God calls His people to a high standard of conduct and expects our obedience.**

This message is what they call a shotgun message. You want to hit the target, holiness and obedience, but you are going to spray a lot of shot over a wide area.

We will continue to follow the standard formula we have followed for all the Amos messages. We begin with,

The Indictments. Verses 6-8 (12)

Verse 6: God follows the same indictment formula 4 +3=7. Seven is the Biblical number of perfection. God is judging

Israel for the entirety of thier sin.

God's first round of indictments against Israel included:

Social Injustice. Verses 6-7a.

Verse 6

The word "righteous" (*saddiq*) doesn't indicate a blameless person, but refers to someone who is "in the right, or has a just cause". "Innocent" may be the best English equivalent of the idea conveyed here.

The poor and needy were being oppressed by the wealthy and they had every right to seek justice.. The did not deserve the treatment they were experiencing.

The poor are bought and sold into slavery. Sometimes they were traded for "silver" reflecting an expensive transaction. At other times, they were traded for a common "pair of sandals"- something of little value. As you can see, the poor and needy were held in very low esteem, if not contempt. They were neglected and abused.

Verse 7a.

The first half of this verse is difficult to translate. The literal translation (from the MT) reads,

"who pant after the dust of the earth on the head of the poor." Longman explains,

..."meaning either that the oppressing classes long to see the poor brought to extreme anguish, or the oppressors are so avaricious that they craved the dust with which the poor had covered their heads. In ancient near eastern culture, pouring dust on one's head signified sorrow (e.g., 2Sam 1.2; Job 2.12)."

When you look at the statement in its whole context and affect, a troubling picture emerges. The rich have trampled down the poor, taking them into slavery, buying and selling them like commodities. They have beaten them down into the dust of the earth and they don't even want them to have the dust that is covering their heads!!!!!!!!!! The picture is one where the poor try to get up out of the dust but the rich "block their path" or push their head back into the dirt.

The bottom line is the rich were exploiting the poor and needy. They were taking what little they had-including their dignity.

Immorality. 7b-8.

The second part of the verse reveals the depth of moral depravity that Israel had sank to. A man and his father "have sexual relations with the same girl." This "profanes the name of God". There really is no need to offer a lengthy explanation here-it is what it is. However, in context realize that God had called Israel to a high level of sexual purity- a level that did not exist in the pagan world. See Leviticus 18-22 for the extensive laws concerning sexual purity among God's people.

You can deduce from the statement that the father and son were more than likely sharing ritual or temple prostitutes as they were "stretched out beside "every altar..." This refers to pagan altars or shrines that dotted the landscape of Israel at the time.

The sexual act is explicit enough, but it gets worse. That the "garments" they were stretched out on were taken as collateral further shows how the rich were taking advantage of the poor. The Law allowed the Israelites to take articles of clothing as collateral or even as payment for loans-with one qualification-the garments had to be returned to the original owner at night so they could stay warm while they slept (Exodus 22.26-27; Deuteronomy 24.12-13).

So, the rich were taking advantage of the poor by indebting them, then they were taking the garments used as collateral and using them to facilitate idolatry, adultery, and fornication. Is it any wonder God pronounced judgment? God shows His distaste for this practice by stating it "profanes His holy name".

To profane (*halal*) means defilement, or perversion. The literal meaning means to slay, pierce or mortally wound someone.

It refers to the carnage of battle (Jer 14.18). It refers to a virgin who has been violated (Lev 21. 7, 14)."

So you can see the impact Israel's sexual sin had on God-they have "pierced, wounded, KILLED, His holy name!

Can you think of any similar situations occurring today in our world today?

Irreverence.

'In the house of their God they drink the wine of those who have been fined".

Wine was sometimes used as currency in the ancient world. Wine was also the primary beverage people drank. It was also used as medicine. To have much wine was considered a sign of prosperity and blessing. The point here seems to be that the rich were taking advantage of the poor, by taking their wine as fines for non-payment of debt and then squandering it by participating in "drinking parties". These were all acts of idolatrous worship.

The Israelites were so far into their depravity that even the most profane acts were no longer taboo, let alone dealt with by the religious leaders. The Hebrew people were called to be a holy people, separated by God as His chosen ones.

Worship was to be conducted in holiness, reverence and respect. Instead, they flaunted their sin as if there would be no consequences.

I'll comment about verse 12 in a minute so just hold on to it for now.

Well, God is angry, there is no doubt. Judgment is inevitable. God next reminds Israel of all that He has done for them.

A Reminder of God's Goodness. Verses 9-12

Not surprisingly, God reminds Israel that she had once been oppressed, down in the dirt, yet he rescued them. He reminds them of four "blessings" He had given them that they had taken lightly:

1. God's granting Israel victory and conquest.

2. God's delivery of Israel from captivity in Egypt.

3. God's gift of "prophets" to deliver His Word to   Israel.

4. God's gift of Nazarites for special blessing to Israel.

Verse 9

The Amorites were the people of Canaan (see Gen 15.16). God reminds the Israelites that He destroyed the Canaanites so that they could claim the Promised Land in which they were now living. Though the Israelites fought the battles, it was the Lord Who gave them the victories.

That God "destroyed the Amorite "fruit and root" points toward their total annihilation.

Verse 10

God reminds Israel of their deliverance from bondage in Egypt. He again reminds that they were given the Amorite lands by His grace.

Verse 11

It's not as if God had not provided prophets to preach His word and expose the nation's sin...It's that they rejected the warnings and now it is too late.

The Nazarites (*nazir-the separate*) took special vows of separation to demonstrate God's desire for His people to be holy and not be partakers of the pagan cultures surrounding them (Numbers 6. 1-12). Samson and Elijah were famous Nazarites. At one time Paul took a temporary Nazarite vow.

Verse 12

Plain and simple, Israel rejected the messages of the prophets. This was the message to repent or judgment was coming. The Israelites also corrupted the Nazarites, therefore destroying their credibility as preachers. The preachers were supposed to be examples of righteousness.

The Nazarites were forbidden to drink wine, or to eat grapes or any part of the grape vine. They were not to cut their hair (Samson was a Nazarite), nor ever touch the dead body of a human or animal.

The prophets were scoffed at (even murdered), and the Nazarites were corrupted-judgment is imminent. God is going to "crush them".

The Punishment. Verses 13-16

Israel will be conquered by an enemy; its army will be utterly defeated.

Verse 13

This is a difficult verse to translate. The ESV attempts to translate the verse and remain faithful to the context, yet misses the point in my opinion. The NASB expresses it better- "Behold, I am weighted down beneath you as a wagon is weighted down when filled with sheaves" (NASB). God is expressing His frustration; Israel has become a "weight" on His shoulders. They are "crushing" his Word and His Heart. The word picture is of an overloaded cart collapsing on its wheels. God is expressing His emotions through the prophet.

Verses 14-16

The swiftest of soldiers will not be able to outrun the coming onslaught.

The strongest of warriors will be overwhelmed and defeated.

Foot soldiers and "light infantry" will be overrun and defeated.

The Calvary will not be able to stop the coming invaders.

Even the bravest, strongest, "elite forces" will fall to the coming invaders raised up by God to mete out His justice in Israel. That they flee "naked" means they will throw down their armor and weapons and run for their lives.

It's not a pretty picture is it? God is very serious about holiness, reverence and social justice. Ok, we get the point. So, how do we apply this to our 21st century Christian lives?

Let's consider:

The Applications.

1. Christians are to care for the poor and needy, especially widows and orphans. This doesn't mean enabling them, but being compassionate and treating them fairly.

2. God has very specific guidelines for human sexuality. Christians honor Him by following them. They sin when they do not.

James combines these two truths to make a very striking statement. James 1.27 reads,

"Religion that is pure and undefiled before God, the Father is this: to visit widows and orphans in their affliction and to keep oneself unstained from the world.

3. God is holy, exalted, supreme and transcendent. We should never worship in irreverent, bawdy, or sinful ways.

4. God has been very good to His people; occasionally you should review all He has done for you.

5. God will only allow His people to sin for so long and to go so far without punishment. His "discipline" is intended to bring us back to Him not drive us further away.

6. For all my preacher friends: When a preacher decides to preach God's word in its full measure, undiluted and historically and grammatically and contextually accurate... people aint going to like it!

-People will leave the church.

-They will try to shut you up, try to get you to compromise.

I had the extreme good fortune to know the late Dr. Wayne Barber. When I met him, he was pastor of Hoffmantown Baptist Church in Albuquerque, New Mexico. Wayne was a "preacher's preacher", and one of the finest Biblical expositors I've met.

Once, during a preaching seminar he told us something that resonates in my mind almost twenty years later. He said, "If you preach the Bible, and stand on Biblical truth, a lot of people will leave your church!"

HIs testimony was that after he had preached two sermons in his new church, people became upset becuase of the content (Biblical, and convicting). So, one of the leaders came to Wayne, and told him that if he preached another sermon similar to the last one, there would be a mass exodus from the church.

Wayne, feared no one but the Lord. So, he said the next Sunday he preached with conviction, and Biblical authority...and maybe just a bit of indignation. He said, "I told them, if they didn't like what I had to say, they were welcome to leave."

Six-hundred people left the fellowship that week! But, you know what? It became a stronger, more God-honoring, and Biblically sound church afterwards.

Not all of you are preachers, yet the application applies to you as well. When a Christian decides he is going to live biblically, that he or she is going to walk with God in purity of heart and holiness of action...you better watch out...people will try to corrupt you. Why? Because they know they aren't living right and unrighteousness loves company.

As we close this chapter, allow me to affirm something. You cannot live righteously without having a personal relationship with Christ. You can't have a personal relationship with Christ without being saved.

If you haven't done so, would you turn to Jesus Christ right now, repent of your sin, ask His forgiveness, "call on His name", and the Bible says when you do that, "you shall be saved. (Romans 10.9-13)

For my Christian friends, let me ask you three questions:

1. What is your attitude toward the poor?

2. How is your moral life?

3. How is your reverence and respect toward God?

I suspect, if you are like me, you have some work to do.

[1]   http://www.828ministries.com/articles/Seeker-Friendly-Irreverenc-by-Anthony-Wade-Faith_God-131009-559.html

CHAPTER EIGHT: HOW GOD DEALS WITH ARROGANCE: AMOS 3

At this point in our study, it might be wise to pause and reflect on the nature of God. Amos is definitely a "prophet of doom", yet careful reading will show that he also speaks of salvation and redemption for Israel. Please remember that God's character is rooted in holiness and justice. Those two characteristics give birth to His love, compassion, mercy, patience, forgiveness, etc. It is easy (especially without the filter of the NT and New Covenant) to see God as an angry, vengeful, Being who is unworthy of our worship and obedience. Nothing could be further from the truth.

The judgments Amos pronounced were centuries in coming. God gave Israel every chance to repent, yet they stubbornly refused.

One must also keep in mind that these judgments are "national" judgments-the nations are being judged and that is irrevocable. However, individuals could still repent and come back to God. They would suffer the national consequences of sin, but could restore their personal relationship with God. This truth remains today.

The major sin God addresses in Amos 3 is the sin of pride. Pride is one of the seven deadly sins. Pride is condemned over and over in the Scriptures. Proverbs 16.18 says, "Pride goes before destruction, and a haughty spirit before a fall". Israel was headed for a very great fall.

God will always "oppose the proud, but shows favor to the humble" (Proverbs 3.34).

Let's divide this passage into four major movements. The first is,

The Lord's Condemnation. Verses 1-3

One of the major issues with Israel was they thought they were untouchable because of their special covenant relationship with God. What they failed to realize was that God's favor on them was conditional upon their obedience to His law. While Israel may have thought that God had suddenly changed His mind about them- this was not the case. God's people had repeatedly, over centuries. changed their mind about God.

Verse 1

Make no mistake; it is the Lord who is speaking. Amos is merely the spokesman.

God also makes it clear that His indictment is against the entire race, not just the Northern kingdom of Israel. God also reminds Israel of His grace and provision in the Exodus. He brought them out of bondage and into the Promised Land (not to mention all of His blessings during the wilderness trek and the conquering of Canaan).

God summons them to listen. The Hebrew word means not only to hear, but to pay attention to what is said, and then act on it. The nation is going down, but the people can still to turn to God for forgiveness.

Verse 2

"Clan" or "family" translates *mishpakhah*, it is used of Israel only here. Patterson and Hill suggest that this was intended to "downgrade" Israel by placing them beside all other nations or (families of the earth).[1]

He does affirm His election of Israel ("I have known only you"), but He isn't happy with them. He, in an emotional phrase, is lumping them together with the pagan nations.

The Lord had "known" only Israel. Know or "to know" translates *yada*. It indicates an intimate special relationship between two people. Here, it is used to describe the covenantal relationship between God and Israel (Gen 12.3, 28.14; Exodus 19. 4-6).

"The word yada bears a special sense of intimacy. Jeremiah 1.5 uses yada in a similar way to God's knowing and consecrating Jeremiah before his birth...it includes the idea of God's sovereign activity whereby the object of that knowledge is set apart or chosen for a divine purpose."[2]

Interestingly, the word translated "punish" *(paqad)* means to inspect, detect a flaw, and then take the appropriate corrective action. "Punishment results if God's inspection reveals a flaw, a fault, some disobedience or sin).[3]

*As a matter of application we might ask, "Is it important that we ask God to inspect our lives periodically (like maybe every single day!)? David wrote,

"Search me, O God, and know my heart; try me and know my anxious thoughts; and see if there be any hurtful way in me, and lead me in the everlasting way." Psalm 139 23-24 (NASB)

Verse 3

Amos asks a rhetorical question-of course not! Literally translated "agreeing to meet" means coming to "terms".[4]

To "walk" (*halak*) together means to be in close association with someone. It carries the idea of cooperation and fellowship. Obviously Israel and God could not "walk" together as God is holy, demands holiness from His people, and they were knee deep in sin. Chiefly, the sin of spiritual arrogance.

I always think of this little story from Chuck Swindoll when I'm around arrogant people, or am tempted to be arrogant myself. He writes,

I got nauseated last week. It wasn't from something I ate, but from someone I met. My out of town travels resulted in a short-term liberal arts education of self-praise to teach me some things I hope I never fully forget. This individual was a widely-traveled, well-educated, much-experienced Christian in his fifties. He is engaged in ministry that touches many lives. He is fundamental in faith, biblical in belief, and evangelical in emphasis. For a number of years he had held a respected position that carries with it a good deal of responsibility and a great deal of time logged in the limelight. Such credentials deserve a measure of respect like the rank on the shoulders of a military officer or the rows of medals on his chest. Both merit a salute in spite of the man in the uniform. In no way do I wish to diminish the significance of his position nor his record of achievement. But my point here is this: "He knew better". He had the ability to correct himself, but he chose to be, quite frankly, a pompous preacher!

You got the distinct impression that when the two of you were together, the more important one was not you. LIttle mistakes irked him. SLight omissions irritated him. Teh attitude of a servant was conspicuous by its absence. It was highly important to him that everyone knw who he was, where he'd been, how he'd done, and what he thought. While everyone else preferred to be on a first name basis (rather than "Reverend" or "Mister") he demanded, "Call *me* Doctor". His voice had a professional tone. As humorous things occurred, he found no reason to smile, and as the group got closer in spirit, he became increasingly more threatened. I confess that I was tempted to short sheet him one night-or to order a Shlitz in his name and have it brought up to his room-or to ask the desk clerk to give him a call about 2;30 A.M. and yell, "Ok, buddy, out of the sack, rise and shine!" But I didn't. Now, I almost wish I had. Just for the fun of watching him squirm!

(From: *Charles R. Swindoll, Growing Strong in the Seasons of Life.*)

One of Israel's major sins was their pride and arrogance. They had the mistaken notion that God would not judge them for wickedness because of their special covenantal relationship. They were very wrong.

what does this means to you?   Let me offer some suggestions:

a. The unsaved cannot assume God will see some good in them and grant salvation through any other means except Christ Jesus.

b. Christians must never become arrogant and sin wantonly knowing that whom the Lord loves, He chastens.

Solomon wrote:

"Everyone who is arrogant in heart is an abomination to the Lord; be assured, he will not go unpunished."

Proverbs 16.5

Rest assured Amos was not a very popular person in Israel. He wasn't like the other prophets who had sinned right along with the people and were now ineffective. He wasn't like the compromised Nazarites. So, God reminds the people that Amos is speaking for Him-and they should listen.

Next up, we see:

The Prophet's Commission. Verses 4-8

Verses 3-6 constitute what is called the "prophetic epigram".

Webster's dictionary defines an epigram as,

1. A short, witty poem expressing a single thought or observation.

2. A concise, clever, often paradoxical statement.

These verses contain seven poetical statements that basically declare if one thing is true, then it is logical that another thing is true. The epigram culminates (7-8) in Amos declaration that the he has no other option, but to speak for God.

Verse 4

If a lion roars...it has caught its prey. A lion will not roar and frighten its victim away.

Applying the same logic: A young lion in the den growls... only when it has caught something.

Verse 5

A bird in a trap...there must have been some bait in it.

If a trap springs...there must be something that triggered it.

Verse 6

If an alarm is sounded (a ram's horn blown in the city indicated an invader was coming or there was some other type of disaster headed their way)...then the people are afraid.

If a disaster ("evil"- meaning some type of calamity) comes...then the Lord allows it.

Now in verses 7-8 Amos comments on and clarifies the epigram.

Verse 7

If the Lord is going to do something...He will reveal (uncover, disclose) it to His "servants the prophets". Amos is not acting on his own accord. Also, he cannot be silent! He must preach, or else face the judgment of God for his disobedience

Do you recall what happened to Jonah when he didn't heed God's call to preach? A lot of spiritual "draft dodgers" have been swallowed up, and spit out over the years!

Verse 8

A lion has roared ...everyone needs to fear.

In case they didn't get it...the Lord has spoken (to Amos) he cannot disobey.

Preachers must preach.   All Christians have the responsibility to "preach the good news" and "make disciples" (Matt 28.19-20).

What happens when we don't?

If a preacher doesn't preach God's word, if he doesn't work hard to deliver the Lord's message to the people, then he sins. Even worse, he will lead the people to sin.

When I first started in ministry one of my mentors made me memorize James 3.1 and he commented on it just about every time we met: "Not many of you should be teachers, my brothers, for you know that we who teach will be judged with greater strictness."

The burden of all prophets and preachers is to preach the Word! Truthfully, all Christians are called to witness for Christ and teach His ways to others.

We cannot ignore the inspired Word of God recorded in Scripture; the Lion of Judah continues to "roar" throughout its pages. We also cannot ignore preachers and teachers who faithfully deliver God's Word. To do so is the height of folly not to mention the very definition of arrogance.

Paul wrote to the Thessalonian church concerning those who would not take instruction:

"As for you brothers, do not grow weary in doing well. If anyone does not obey what we say in this letter, take note of that person, and have nothing to do with him, that he may be ashamed. Do not regard him as an enemy, but warn him as a brother."

2 Thessalonians 3. 14-15

The Israelites thought they were superior to anyone else. They thought they were untouchable. They looked down on other races and ethnic groups.

By this point in history, they had become bigots of the highest order. God brings them down a notch. In verses 9-11. He makes:

The Sobering Comparison. Verses 9-11

Verse 9

Amos calls two of Israel's arch-enemies to witness their sin and rebellion against God. Egypt had enslaved Israel even calling for their baby boys to be slaughtered at birth (Exodus 1). Egypt was also home to great immorality and idolatry. They worshipped a plethora of gods, including the sun and the moon.

Ashdod was a Philistine city. The Philistines were traditional enemies of Israel. They were a violent, warlike people (remember Goliath?). Their main deity was the god, Dagon. Dagon was a half-man, half fish.

That God would summon these two particularly evil nations to witness the evil in Israel shows something of the state of affairs in Israel. Dr.'s Patterson and Hill comment that there was a two-fold purpose for God's actions here,

"First, it served to spotlight the depth of corruption in Israel by having nations that were the epitome of evil to judge their misconduct. Second, it showed that covenant law was not the only criterion what would condemn Israel's behavior; by any standards of human decency they stood guilty as charged."

There is turmoil and oppression in Samaria (capital city of Israel at that time). Turmoil and oppression seem to be a cause and effect situation.

Samaria represented the rich and influential elites of the Northern kingdom. Apparently, and certainly no suprise,they oppressed the poor. As a consequence there was great social upheaval and unrest. Chaos would accurately describe the situation as observed by God.

Verse 10

Things had disintegrated to the point where the people were incapable of doing "right". Right translates (n'koha) and means "straight". Used in the moral sense it means to be upright, fair, holy, etc. Israel was "crooked". They had forgotten what was morally correct and had been in sin so long they no longer perceived it as such.

*Is the USA in the same moral condition as Israel was in Amos' time?

They were full of "violence and destruction". To God's great displeasure, it was directed towards their own people which made it even worse.

Verse 11

God pronounces the method and means of the judgment. Not through a "natural" disaster, or plague, or diseases-but through a conqueror. This would be the Assyrian army under Tiglath-pileser III circa 732 (Cf. 2 Kings 15-16; 1 Chronicles 5).

I was dealing with some very difficult issues in a church one time. There were so many problems, there was adultery, drug use, stealing, it was just a mess. Of course no pastor had ever bothered to confront the issues and it was dumped in my lap.

I was asking my dad for advice on how to handle these things. Now, my dad is a very calm easy going guy (I unfortunately did not inherit these traits). But when I laid it all out he was so surprised, he said, "Good night son, even lost people have better morals and behavior than those people!" God forbid that is ever said about you or your church.

Don't get lost in the narrative. Let me remind you of something:

Through Amos, God accused the Israelites of being morally and spiritually inferior to the pagan nations that surrounded them.

It's a sad fact of our day that people, even Christian people, have, through neglect and rebellion, forgotten how to live holy and acceptable lives. Living in open and unrepentant sin shows an arrogance that will eventually lead to ruin.

Since the Israelites were acting worse than their pagan neighbors, God gives them a glimpse of their future. It isn't a pretty sight. Let's consider now:

The Fearful Conclusion. Verses 12-15

Verse 12

God is not predicting Israel's salvation here. He is being sarcastic. The metaphor suggests that the "sheep" is dead and all the "shepherd" can do is salvage a few bits and pieces of torn body parts. The nation will be totally devastated. However, there is a "hint" of remnant theology here.

A few "bits and pieces" of Israel will remain and God will bring them out of exile and they will rebuild the nation.

The latter part of verse 12 is difficult to translate. There may be a reference here to a colony of Israelites in Damascus (capital of Syria) that will not escape God's judgment (KJV reflects this). If this is the case, it doesn't affect the meaning.

Those rich oppressive Israelites will be conquered and

taken captive carried on bits and pieces of their former wealth. Couches and beds were signs of wealth and shameful opulence.

One of the best explanations of this verse comes from Donald J. Sunukjian,

Some of Amos' hearers might have objected to this announcement, insisting that somehow the Israelites would be saved. The word "saved" (usually translated "rescued" or" delivered" in NIV) often described God's delivering or sparing of Israel...This revealed the mistaken belief of Amos' hearers that God would surely rescue them from such a catastrophe. To dispel this false hope, Amos repeated what the Lord said: any "saving" of Israel would be like a shepherd saving a couple of leg bones or part of an ear from the jaws of a wild animal. These little "bits" of rescued evidence were to prove that a shepherd had not stolen or sold one of the sheep, but that it indeed had been torn by a beast of prey...The rescued shin bones and the tip of an ear only proved that rescue had come too late and the animal was a total loss.

Those Israelites in Samaria (and perhaps Damascus) who dissolutely lounged on their beds and couches should not dismiss Amos' message with vague assurances of deliverance. Israel (the nation) would be totally and savagely devoured.

Verse 13

This particular chapter reads somewhat like a courtroom scene. There is a crime, a judge and witnesses are called.

Now, the "witnesses" are called to "testify" against Israel.

Verse 14

"Altars of Bethel" refer to Israel's religious sins. Jeroboam had erected golden calves in the area of Bethel and God intended for them to be destroyed. (Cf. 1 Kings 12.32; 13.2; 2 Kings 23. 15-16). In Jewish law (1 Kings 1.50) one could run to the "horns of the altar" grasp them and be spared a death penalty. Metaphorically God is saying you won't be able to run to your false gods for help during the Day of Judgment.

Verse 15

Those who could afford summer and winter homes were obviously the wealthy oppressors. God is going to take them away.

Only the very rich could afford ivory. Ivory was used to decorate their opulent mansions. Even these monuments will be destroyed or plundered in the coming invasion.

Once God judges Israel there will be very little left to salvage.

In the same way, this is a frightening prospect for Christians who have fallen into sin. When you refuse to repent and get right with God you will still be saved, though you may be "torn up" a bit. Hebrews 10.31 reads,

"It is a terrifying thing to fall into the hands of the living God."

The worst act of arrogance and pride is to refuse the free gift of salvation offered by the Lord Jesus Christ. When Christ tugs at your heart and you turn Him away you are telling Him that you don't need Him or want Him. You are telling Him that His death on the cross doesn't mean anything to you. You are telling Him you would rather spend eternity in hell than spend it in heaven with the saints. When you refuse Christ you tell Him you much prefer your sin than to be forgiven. That you would rather live in bondage than freedom. That's pride...and it'll lead to your ruin.

Drop the pride, come Christ.

[1] Patterson and Hill, 175

[2] Longman and Garland, 381

[3] Ibid

[4] HCBS, 1496

CHAPTER 9: THE DANGER OF DECADENCE AMOS 4

We live in an age of decadence. Pro athletes are making millions to play a game. Counting endorsements Tiger Woods grossed a reported 156.2 million dollars in 2013. Robert Downey Jr. was paid $75 million to star in the last Avengers movie. The average salary for an elementary school teacher in Kentucky? $50, 767...there is something bad wrong with this picture.

It seems like we live in a day when luxury, power, and money have become the official "gods" of the USA.

There is great danger in decadence. What do I mean by decadence? Let me give you the working definition: Decadence is moral or cultural decline as characterized by excessive indulgence in pleasure or luxury. Are we or are we not surrounded by it?

Israel had fallen into extreme decadence. They had forgotten their God. They were worshipping idols, exploiting one another, and indulging their every carnal desire.

There are consequences for an individual, a nation, and a church that falls into decadence- none of them are good.

In this section of the book, Amos prophesizes three major consequences of decadence. First,

The Depreciation of Moral and
Social Responsibility. Verses 1-3

Amos refers to the wealthy pampered women of Samaria, which was the capital of Israel at the time, as *cows of Bashan*. If you want to talk about a brave prophet, or one who feared no one but the Lord, there you are! He has just called the wives of the wealthy and powerful upper class men of Israel a bunch of heifers! Try that brother! That'll get you voted out of your church real quick!

The area of Bashan was a very fertile pastureland just north of the Sea of Galilee. Its cattle were famous for being well fed and plump. You might compare the "cows of Bashan" with Japanese Kobe beef. I read th other day that Japanese farmers feed Kobs beef beer, and give them massages!

He accuses Israel of oppressing the poor and crushing the needy. They had exploited the poor for their own gain. They had taken their clothing as surety and not returned it.

They had charged outrageous interest on loans. They went out of their way to mistreat the poor and needy: and God wasn't happy about it.

Amos' imagery is that of the decadent, overfed wives, lying on couches in fine homes, gorged on fine food and drink while the lower classes (whom they exploited for wealth) barely survive just outside their windows.

Their husbands should have been noble. They should have insisted on modest, godly living but they indulged their spoiled wives' every whim. God isn't terribly pleased with the situation.

Verses 2-3

The Lord swears by His most important attribute: His holiness. There is nothing, or no one greater to swear by. He has spoken, the judgment is irrevocable. God cannot lie. He cannot allow sin to go unpunished. He will not allow this decadence to continue.

"They" are the Assyrian troops that will ransack Israel, destroy her walls (breaches) and drag off even these spoiled noble women into slavery. Notice the metaphor. They will drag off the decadent rich indignantly, like a fisherman who hooks a fish and drags it in.

It also carries the idea of slavery. Archeologists have uncovered paintings from ancient Assyria that showed them leading captives around by ropes attached to rings in their noses.

It's plain to see that God hates it when the rich and the powerful abuse the poor and helpless.

We also see that He hates sloth and gluttony and decadent indulgence.

Jesus tells us a parable that illustrates this point. Allow me to share a paraphrase from the Redneck Revised Standard Version:

He tells us that there was a rich man who had everything. He lived in a mansion. He wore Armani suits. His shoes were handmade by John Lobe. He ate the finest food prepared by the best chefs.

The only blemish on his otherwise perfect life was this beggar named Lazarus. Lazarus had some type of terrible disease that caused his body to break out in nasty running sores. Every day somebody brought Lazarus and laid him right in front of the gates to the rich man's driveway. When the security guards came to run him off he said, "All I want is a few crumbs of bread so I won't starve to death." They just pulled him aside and tried to get back inside before the dogs came and licked at his sores. Yet the rich man gave him nothing. This went on day after day until Lazarus finally died.

But Lazarus was a righteous man and the "angels

carried him to heaven to be with the Lord. Lazarus was given a mansion to live in. He was given the finest clothes to wear. His skin was no longer covered with sores, but was smooth and handsome. He never went hungry for he ate of the tree of life, and drank from the river of life.

Well the rich man dies as well. Jesus tells us his fate was a little different. He woke up in hell, surrounded by flames and torment.

Worst of all, he could see over into heaven and there was Lazarus, who he despised, sitting with the Lord living in luxury.

Jesus tells us he cried out to God for mercy, "Lord, sent Lazarus down here with just a drop of water on the tip of his finger to cool my tongue! I'm burning up in these flames!"

But the Lord said, "Lazarus is busy living the good life! He had it rough on earth, remember?" You wouldn't lift a hand to end his suffering. You had it good when you were on earth, I expected you to live modestly, to help the poor and needy, but you didn't. Now you must suffer. There is a great chasm, a grand canyon, between heaven and hell. No one here can come to you."

That's a pretty scary scenario. It's one that many decadent, immoral powerful rich people will live out for themselves some day.

Please understand, being wealthy and influential is not a sin. God blesses many people with material abundance, status, and power.

However, He hates it when the wealthy and powerful oppress or exploit the poor in their quest for more wealth. He also desires that His people live modestly, and invest their resources in benevolent ministries.

Jesus makes it very plain that:

"No servant can serve two masters, for either he will hate the one and love the other, or he will be devoted to the one and despise the other. You cannot serve God and money." Luke 16.13

One of the most harmful things about decadence is that it tends to display itself in all areas of your life. Once immoral indulgence starts it can spread like wildfire into your thought life, your work life, and your social life, and even into your spiritual life. This is exactly what had happened in Israel. The excessive decadence of the people had led them into outright idolatry. The second sign of a decadent person or nation is:

The Decline of Genuine Worship. Verses 4-5

Let me set these verses in context before we look at them. The problem with worshipping at Bethel and Gilgal is that they were not the prescribed locations for worship. The Israelites were supposed to take their offerings and sacrifices to the Temple in Jerusalem. Yet, King Jeroboam had ordered worship sites to be constructed in these two areas as "alternative" places and had even ordained his own priests. This was clearly against the Law of Moses. To make matters worse, he also placed Canaanite idols at the sites. Among the many idols he put there was a golden calf. You would have thought Israel would have learned the first time the problem this particular idol could cause!

So what you have is this very odd mix of trying to fulfill covenantal worship mixed with pagan worship and idolatry: it would never work!

Verses 4-5

God is being very sarcastic here. He mockingly tells them, "Hey, come on to Bethel and sin and sin away. Go on to Gilgal and do it even more."

He tells them that even if they brought sacrifices every morning and tithed every three days (which they were not required to do under the Law) it wouldn't make any difference.

They were wicked, their hearts were not right, they boasted and bragged about their decadent worship: He was disgusted with it all.

God is telling us something here, you can "do" all kinds of religious spiritual stuff, you can be extravagant in giving, in serving, but if your heart isn't right, if you are doing it for the wrong reasons: God isn't pleased. In fact, it makes Him mad!

I fear a lot of our worship today has become disingenuous. It just isn't genuine. We make it too familiar; we forget that we are in the presence of the Holy One. We come with way too much sin, too much baggage, too much cultural bias, too much familiarity with the sacred. Often times I fear we tread too close to the line of practical idolatry. A.W. Tozer wrote in an essay entitled, *Worship, The Missing Jewel,*

Worship, I say, rises or falls with our concept of God; that is why I do not believe in these half converted cowboys who call God the Man Upstairs. I do not think they worship at all because their concept of God is unworthy of God and unworthy of them. And if there is one terrible disease in the Church of Christ, it is that we do not see God as great as He is.

We are too familiar with God. Communion with God is one thing; familiarity with God is quite another.

I don't even like (and this may hurt some of your feelings—but they'll heal) I don't even like to hear God called "You." "You" is a colloquial expression. I can call a man "you," but I ought to call God "Thou" and "Thee."

Now I know these are old Elizabethan words, but I also know that there are some things too precious to cast lightly away and I think that when we talk to God we ought to use the pure, respectful pronouns.

Also I think we ought not to talk too much about

Jesus just as Jesus. I think we ought to remember who He is. "He is thy Lord; and worship thou Him." And though He comes down to the lowest point of our need and makes Himself accessible to us as tenderly as a mother to her child, still don't forget that when John saw Him–that John who had lain on His bosom when John saw Him he fell at His feet as dead.

To which, we all should repent, and a hearty "Amen"!

Beloved we need to remember Who it is that we are worshipping, and what His requirements are for true worshippers. Our decadent lifestyle can lead us to decadent, self-centered, worldly worship. We cannot afford to mix anything with our worship that would remove the focus on God. There is plenty of room for creativity in worship that stays within Biblical bounds.

There are plenty of ways to worship that don't require a dog and pony show to please or entertain people. I could go on with this but I'll stop here.

God does not accept worship that is insincere, improper or uninformed. Jesus said that we must worship in "spirit" and in "truth" (John 4. 24). Any superficial act of worship, no matter how grand means nothing to God.

The writer of Hebrews put it this way,

"Therefore let us be grateful for receiving a kingdom that cannot be shaken, and thus let us offer to God acceptable worship, with reverence and awe, for our God is a consuming fire." Hebrews 12. 28-2

Yes, our God is a consuming fire, but He is also a patient God. When His people become decadent He will warn them, discipline them to get them to repent and get back on the right track.

One of the problems with decadence is that the more we indulge in sin, the less likely we are to heed God's warnings, no matter how severe they may be.

This is exactly what we find in the last portion of this chapter. The third and most disastrous result of decadence is:

The Disregard of God's Discipline. Verses 6-14

God did everything He could to get Israel's attention, to turn them back to Him, but they were so decadent they just didn't get it.

It's important to note here that God is following up on His covenant agreement with Israel. He warned them if they fell into sin that these types of judgments would come. But they had silenced the prophets. They had compromised the Nazarites. There was no one left to warn them. Now, all Amos can do is tell them they have missed their opportunity to repent.

In the following verses, Amos describes the many ways God disciplined Israel, to no god effect:

Verse 6-famine

Verses 7-8-drought

Verse 9- Blight and mildew

Verse 10- pestilence, in the form some type of locust or

bug

Verse 11- War, terrorism

Verse 12, is frightening,   The window for national repentance has closed. Now, they need to prepare for judgment.

Verse 13:   Here God reaffirms His sovereignty.   He reminds Israel of just who they have offended with their decadence.

I originally wrote this series in 2013. Think about how many "incidents" have happened since these I listed back then:

Mudslides: the Washington mudslide death toll is up to 30.

Tornadoes: In Moore Oklahoma's 2013 24 killed and over 3,000 injured.

Storms: Hurricane Sandy: 285 fatalities.

Floods: 2103 flooding in Colorado took 144 lives.

Drought: The western US (especially CA) is in a terrible drought.

Economic downturn

Wars: Afghanistan, Ukraine (we will be involved at some point). Read Ezekiel: when you see Russia and China forming alliances...look out

Terrorist attacks: Boston Marathon bombing killed 3 injured over 200

Immoral and Unethical government...you know it's true

Earthquakes- There were some severe ones this week.   Don't forget the massive one in Haiti that claimed approximately 300,000 lives.

Shootings at schools and military bases

Don't you just want to yell, "What's it going to take?"

I'm not a prophet or the son of a prophet but I'm very afraid for our nation. I think we may be at the stage where God's judgment is irrevocable.

Many times we can become so decadent that even God's most drastic attempts to correct us go unheeded. It is wise to evaluate your circumstances to discern what God is saying and adjust your life accordingly.

"Remember therefore from where you have fallen; repent and do the works you did at first. If not, I will come to you and remove your lampstand from its place unless you repent." Revelation 2.5

Decadence begins with a moral decline; it progresses to depreciated worship and culminates with disregard for God's discipline.

Every person ought to take stock of their lives to see if decadence has slipped in. Is there any "decay" in the moral life? Are you tender-hearted toward the poor and powerless?

What is your attitude in worship?

Is God trying to get your attention? How are you responding to His "chastening" hand?

CHAPTER 10: SEEK THE LORD AND LIVE AMOS 5. 1-17

God hates sin. God loves sinners, but He despises their sin. Because God hates sin He must eventually judge sinners. Thankfully, He has given us a way to escape His judgment. We can turn to the Lord Jesus Christ, believe in Him, repent of our sin, receive His gracious forgiveness and be spared God's wrath. All humans have a choice to make: we can die in our sins or we can seek the Lord and live.

That is the message of this passage. Actually, it is the message of the entire book of Amos. Seek the Lord and live.

Let's take minute to review Amos' prophecy, before we move into these final chapters.

Amos prophesied during the 8th century BC. During that time the nation of Israel was divided into two kingdoms: Israel to the North and Judah to the South.

This was a time of relative peace and prosperity for both nations, especially for Israel. The people, God's chosen people, took God's blessing for granted, forgot their covenant requirements and had fallen into sin. Their sin was extensive.

They had become idolatrous, inhospitable, immoral, and exploited the poor. It would be wise for you to take the time to go back and read chapters 1-4 to refresh your memory.

God sent many prophets to Israel to warn her to repent of her sin, or else He would judge them severely. For the most part they were ignored. God's means of judgment would be the massive Assyrian army that would invade the nation, kill most of the people, and take the others into exile. However, in His mercy, God was holding the Assyrians back, allowing Israel time to repent: even though He knew they wouldn't.

One unlikely prophet was the fellow that wrote this book: Amos. Amos was a herdsman and fig farmer from the backwater town of Tekoa. He was not a "professional" prophet, yet God sent this country boy to the cities of the North to preach this message of impending judgment, and to call the people to repentance. We know from history that they rejected his message.

Amos certainly carries a message for we who live in the 21st century. It doesn't take a prophet to look around and see conditions in our world are very similar to the ones in Amos' time. All around us we see gross immorality, idolatry and injustice. We see these things in our nation, in our homes and sadly, even in our churches.

Could it be that God is getting ready to send judgment? The only proper thing we can do today is to heed the Word of God. If we are to be spared, we need to "seek the Lord and live!

This passage is structured like an ancient Hebrew funeral "dirge". It is a sad mournful song that speaks of death and destruction, but also interjects words of hope as well. The "dirges" consisted of four parts. The first part is,

The Description of the Tragedy. Verses 1-3

Amosprovides a two- part description of the coming tragedy:

(1.) The fall of the house of Israel. Verses 1-2

Amos sings of the fall of Israel in the past tense, even though it is a future event. This shows us the certainty of God's judgment. The Hebrew word translated "fallen" (*napal*) "evokes pictures of defeat in battle."[1] It isn't a discrepancy that God declares "Israel" will never rise again for we know she indeed does. However, the Northern kingdom as a "stand alone" nation will never rise again. Israel, in the restoration period, becomes one unified nation with Jerusalem serving as the capital.

Israel (the northern kingdom) is a "virgin" and her young life is being cut off before she has a chance to marry and produce offspring.

This is an especially vivid metaphor. Bearing children was seen as God's favor and blessing upon a woman.

A barren woman was looked down on by society. She was considered to be cursed by God. God uses this imagery to show Israel's utter defeat and humiliation.

God will "abandon" (forsake-divorce) Israel because Israel has violated the covenantal provisions (Mainly social injustice and idolatry. Cf. Deuteronomy 32. 15-20).

Jeremiah wrote in his lament,

"How the Lord in His anger has set the daughter of Zion under a cloud! He has cast down from heaven to earth the splendor of Israel; He has not remembered His footstool in the day of His anger." Lamentations 2.1

(2.) The promise of a remnant. Verse 3

This is a scene of devastation. Israel's mighty army will be defeated and humiliated. Ninety percent of the army will be killed in battle! But, there is a glint of hope here. A remnant will be preserved (though a small one). God will not break His promises to the Patriarchs even though Israel has fallen into such a backslidden state.

We find a rather graphic illustration of the condition of the remnant in chapter three, verse 12:

Thus says the Lord, "As the shepherd rescues from the mouth of the lion two legs, or a piece of an ear, so shall the people of Israel who dwell in Samaria be rescued, with the corner of a couch and part of a bed."

Some will survive, but they will be in rough shape.

Isaiah spoke of this as well,

"For though your people Israel be as the sand of the sea," only a remnant of them will return." Destruction is decreed, overflowing with righteousness." Isaiah 10.22

Is there any hope? With God there is always hope! The second movement in a funeral dirge is known as,

The Summons to Respond.

Verses 4-6; 14-15

The Lord demands two responses of Israel. They are to:

(1.) Seek the Lord and live. Verses 4-6

Verse 4

The Lord gives the only possible hope for survival...they are to "seek Me (God) and live. To "seek" *(darash)* means to 'turn to God in trust and confidence.' This is what individuals must do in order to survive the coming judgment. The grammar of this statement suggests that "if" the whole nation would return to God, He, in turn, would relent. But, God knows this will not happen. However, we cannot ignore that God extends grace and mercy to repentant sinners, even if the nation as a whole continues in rebellion.

Dr.'s Longman and Garland comment,

"In this light, it is hardly correct to say that Amos confronts the people only with doom.

He holds out a gracious invitation to them, but he expects only calamity because he knows they will not repent. His invitation may be instrumental in leading some of the people to seek the Lord; thus it contributes to the establishment of the remnant."[2]

Don't ever lose sight of this truth! The nation, actually the entire world is going down, read the Bible, it's an inevitable event...but you don't have to go down with it. You can turn to Jesus Christ in faith and repentance and LIVE. Unfortunately, most people run to something other than God when calamity strikes. Look at,

Verses 5-6

Bethel, Gilgal and Beersheba were centers of worship and destinations for pilgrims. This was a perversion because God declared that the temple in Jerusalem was the only authorized place for sacrifices. The worship in these unauthorized places was corrupted and was considered worthless in God's eyes (see chapter 4). They had become places of idolatry and immorality. God warns the Israelites not to return to this worthless worship, but to turn their hearts back toward Him. These cities and their people with their evil ways were going to be destroyed.

Once again Amos appeals to the Israelites to "seek" or "return" to God or face the consequences.

The "House of Joseph" refers to the northern kingdom which was mainly composed of the tribe of Ephraim, the son of Joseph. God's judgment is described as a consuming fire that no one can put out.

Bethel, the site of idolatrous and unworthy worship is especially singled out for destruction. This shows the Lord's hatred of idolatry and heartless worship.

Now, find verses 14-15. Here we find the second thing Israel should do if they want to escape God's judgment. They are to:

(2.) Seek good, and not evil. Verses 14-15

Amos calls the Israelites to return to good, to return to their covenantal obligations, and only then they may live. The word translated live (*chayah*) can mean to "restore to life", or have abundant life. In can even refer to "eternal life". Once again we see that God is willing to bless Israel if they would only turn from their wickedness, but they won't. Also, we see the idea of personal repentance here. Individuals who return to doing good can lay claim to the Lord's favor.

In verse 15 Amos is being dramatic, if not a bit sarcastic. Of course if the remnant of Israel repents of their sin, God will be gracious to them.

It is important to note something here. Notice the last part of verse 14: ..."it may be that the God of hosts, will be with you as you have said".

They thought that God was going to bless them and ignore their sin! They thought the party was never going to end! Not much has changed today has it? People have become so arrogant, so confident, that they think they are beyond God's reach. Or worse yet, they think God owes them something. Let me give you an example:

Someone gave me an article this week that has a quote from former NYC mayor Michael Bloomberg. Read this, and be amazed at this arrogance and disregard for God:

'I'm telling you if there is a God, when I get to heaven I'm not stopping to be interviewed. I am heading straight in. I have earned my place in heaven. It's not even close. [3]

We need to pray for this man to be saved. I shudder to think of his "interview" with God.

Isaiah tells us exactly how we need to respond to the summons of God:

"Seek the Lord while He may be found; call upon Him

while He is near; let the wicked forsake his way, and the unrighteous man his thoughts; let him return to the Lord, that He may have compassion on him, and to our God for He will abundantly pardon." Isaiah 55. 6-7

The third "stanza" of Amos' funeral dirge consists of:

The Direct Address to the Fallen. Verses 7-13

God's address to the fallen can be sectioned under three general headings. The first, let's call:

(1.) The depths of Israel's corruption. Verse 7

This serves as a transition in the song. In the following "stanza" (8-13), God compares His righteousness with the wickedness of Israel. He begins with a strong condemnation of Israel.

They have turned "justice" to "wormwood" which is an extremely bitter plant. In Scripture, wormwood symbolizes bitterness, evil, and hardship (Cf. Pro 5.4, Lam 3.15). Justice is sweet and comforting, but the corrupt judges of Israel have ruined it. Metaphorically speaking the Israelites have taken righteousness and "thrown it into the dirt".

Next, Amos calls us to contrast the depths of Israel's wickedness with:

(2.) The heights of the Lord's Glory.

Verses 8-9

Instead of running to idols that are nothing more than stone and wood and metal, powerless and without life; Israel should run to God. He is not only real and living, but He is sovereign over all people and all things. He:

1.   Made the constellations.

2.   He establishes night and day.

3.   He "summoned" the seas and oceans to cover

the land. (This may be an allusion to the Flood in Noah's time: an act of judgment).

4.   He is sovereign in human affairs. This is exemplified in the fact that He overthrows military strongholds (fortresses) and armies.   This is a clear reference to Israel's falling to a military conqueror raised up by God to be His "arm of judgment".

Since God created all, and is over all, He has the authority, and the right to pronounce this judgment against Israel. Now let's look at:

(3.) The consequences of Israel's sin.

Verses 10-13

Verse 10

Legal proceedings most often took place at the city gates. The Israelites have so perverted justice that they hate anyone who would make righteous (fair and impartial and moral) decisions in legal proceedings. If anyone dares speak on behalf of the innocent or the mistreated they were "despised".

Do we not see this happening in our nation and the rest of the world today? There are a lot of things before the courts, but there is very little justice.

Verses 11-12

Israel's oppression and mistreatment of the poor kindle the wrath of God. The wealthy in Israel have taxed the poor to the point of absurdity. They have "trampled" them.

At the same time, the wealthy have taken their "ill-gotten gains" and built mansions of stone and cultivated lush vineyards. Two luxuries they will not get to enjoy much longer. Soon a conqueror will live in their fine houses and drink wine from their lush vineyards.

The crimes and sins of Israel cannot be counted,

there are just too many.

Oppression, bribery, injustice in the "court system"; these things are mere drops in the bucket of Israel's evil, but they seem particularly offensive to God.

Is this not a strong message to all those who serve in the public sector? Should not all government officials take note? Shouldn't anyone who cheats another take notice of the Lord's Word here? I think so.

Verse 13

The wise or prudent find it best to keep silent. The idea is that protest may lead to greater injustices against the oppressed and the poor.

God speaks frankly. When judgment comes, when the invaders destroy the nation, when barbaric Assyrian soldiers sit in Israelite houses and drink their wine, they cannot scratch their heads and think, "Why did this happen?"

What does this mean to modern people? Well, God hasn't minced any words. He has spoken plainly about sin and its consequences.

He has also shown us the way to escape those consequences. Paul sums this up in one short verse,

"For the wages of sin is death, but the free gift of God is eternal life in Christ Jesus our Lord." Romans 6.23

The final "stanza" of this funeral dirge is:

The Call to Mourning. Verses 16-17

Amos holds out no hope for national repentance. The Lord of Hosts (Commander of angelic armies) declares that there will be nothing but mourning when He judges Israel. Notice the mourning of all sectors of the nation:

1.   The public squares.

2.   The city streets.

3.   In the countryside.

Those skilled in lamentation were the "professional mourners". One could hire them to mourn for the deceased (Cf. Jer 9.17-22; Matt 9.23). In Amos' culture the act of mourning bordered on hysteria. The mourners will have a lot of business when God judges the nation.

This is a terrible scene of chaos, of destruction of people running and crying and begging for help-and none comes! This is the emotional state that will be produced as a result of God's judgment.

We've all seen on television the chaos after the terrorist attacks at the World Trade Center, the Pentagon and the crash in Pennsylvania. Remember the loud crying? Remember the smoke and the debris in the air?   Remember the people running and yelling and crying? That's the scene Amos predicts for Israel when God brings judgment.

Anyone reading this, who doesn't take God's judgment seriously, needs to wake up!

Isaiah gives an even more graphic description of this event,

Wail, for the day of the Lord is near; as destruction from the Almighty it will come! Therefore all hands will be feeble, and every human heart will melt. They will be dismayed: pangs and agony will seize them; they will be in anguish like a woman in labor. They will look aghast at one another; their faces will be aflame. Isaiah 13.6-8

When God brings judgment against a nation it will encompass all sectors of society. From the public square, the city streets, to the rural countryside; the people will mourn. It's also notable that even the righteous will suffer due to the sins of the unrighteous.

This was my conclusion to the original message:

Tomorrow is Memorial Day. It is a day when we here in the United States pause, and remember those who died while serving in our armed forces. We all owe those men and women a great debt for we wouldn't enjoy the rights and privileges we have without their dedicated service and sacrifice.

Any time that aggressors have threatened or attacked our nation, our troops have bravely answered the call of duty. Many, many, have laid down their lives for our nation, and we are grateful.

The Bible tells us that there is one who laid down His life for every person, in every nation. That is the Lord Jesus Christ. He died to pay the penalty for sin. He suffered and was crucified to satisfy the wrath of God. Of course, He did something very special three days later: He rose again! And because of that you can be saved. You can have eternal life. You can have peace and joy and hope now, and a glorious eternal existence in heaven.

You see God still hates sin, and yes, He still loves sinners; that's why He has made it possible through Jesus for you to escape His coming judgment. One day, He will pour out His final fury on this earth and it will be completely destroyed. The only way to survive is to trust Jesus Christ as your Lord and Savior. Have you? You do not want to die in your sins and go to hell. So the appeal of this chapter is: Will you seek the Lord and live?

[1] Anderson and Freedman, 1989:474 As quoted in Patterson and Hill, 184

[2] Longman and Garland, 396

[3] As quoted in American Hunter: June 2014, page 18

CHAPTER 11:
THE DANGER OF
TAINTED WORSHIP
AMOS 5. 18-27

God is very serious when it comes to worship! He is a jealous God and demands our complete devotion and loyalty. The first commandment in the Decalogue, the Ten Commandments (the unchanging moral law), is:

"You shall have no other gods before me." (Exodus 20.3)

God is also very serious when it comes to how and why we worship. God really isn't impressed with grand displays of worship if your heart is full of wickedness, and sin reigns in your life. Truthfully, it is better not to worship at all than it is to offer God tainted worship.

Tainted, impure, "polluted" worship was one of Israel's main sins that had provoked God to judgment.

Tainted worship is the sin God moves Amos to preach against in this passage. Let's set the stage for Amos' message by reading from the 2 Kings 17. I think you will see the situation very clearly:

In the ninth year of Hoshea, the king of Assyria captured Samaria, and he carried the Israelites away to Assyria and placed them in Halah, and on the Habor, the river of Gozan, and in the cities of the Medes.

And this occurred because the people had sinned against the Lord their God, who brought them out of the land of Egypt from under the hand of Pharaoh king of Egypt, and had feared other gods and walked in the customs of the nations whom the Lord drove out before the people of Israel, and in the customs that the kings of Israel had practiced. And the people of Israel did secretly against the Lord their God things that were not right. They built for themselves high places in all their towns, from watchtower to fortified city. They set up for themselves pillars and Asherim on every high hill and under every green tree, and there they made offerings on all the high places, as the nations did whom the Lord carried away before them. And they did wicked things, provoking the Lord to anger, and they served idols, of which the Lord had said to them, "You shall not do this." (Now here is where Amos and his contemporaries come in) Yet the Lord warned Israel and Judah by every prophet and every seer, saying, 'Turn from your evil ways and keep my commandments and my statutes, in accordance with all the Law that I commanded your fathers, and that I sent to you by my servants the prophets.

But they would not listen, but were stubborn, as their fathers had been who did not believe in the Lord their God. (Verses 6-13)

This is the spiritual situation in which we find Amos prophesying to Israel. Judgment had not come, yet...but it was coming!

The eternal truth we find in this passage is that God will not accept tainted worship. You simply cannot love worldly, carnal things more than you love God.   There is a day of reckoning coming.

The Lord Jesus holds us accountable for each facet of our lives- including our worship. If we want to please our Lord, then our worship must be pure, and motivated by our love for, and fear of Him.

The Holy Spirit, speaking through Amos gives us three things to think about in this message . He speaks to us about two dangers and then gives us a command to follow. The first danger is:

The Danger of False Security. Verses 18-20

Verse 18

The day of the Lord in the theological mind of the Jews would be the day when the Messiah came to earth, conquered all His foes (ironically also the foes of Israel) , and established an earthly kingdom in Jerusalem. This is what they longed for. This would be the day of their consolation. This would be the day when God would fulfill all of His promises to them.

What they failed to consider was that they would also be held accountable for keeping their covenant agreements and living pure lives. As we have already learned, they had fallen into the worst kinds of sin.

Amos is the first of the prophets to use the term "The Day of the Lord" as a particular judgment of God against Israel. It will carry this meaning from this point on. The Israelites longed for THE DAY OF THE LORD, but the day of the Lord they would soon face would not bode well for them.

"Woe to you", he says. Woe translates the Hebrew word *hoy* it is a term used to lament a person's death. Similar to the funeral dirge. It is used to indicate impending doom and destruction on a grand scale. He asks, "Why in the world are you excited about the day of the Lord?"

Amos uses some rather unsettling metaphors to shatter Israel's false security.

Verses 19-20

Amos uses poetical imagery here:

1. The day won't be a day of "light", or joy for rebellious Israel. It will be dark and depressing.

2. Instead of deliverance (like running from a lion) they will only face God's wrath and judgment (confronting a bear). The imagery intimates that just when Israel thinks they are safe, they are home free: Wham!

3. A man feels like he has made it safely home only to be bitten by a poisonous snake inside the house.

Israel had developed a false sense of security and they had a rude awakening coming.

Well over 30 years ago I had to take a course in Terrorism/ Counter terrorism as part of my college degree. At that time the hot beds of terrorism were Northern Ireland, Israel, and Central Africa.

I remember our professor teaching that the United States would NEVER face a terrorist attack because of the strength of our military and tight security.

A few years later I was in a terrorism/counter terrorism training course. The instructor told us that after America's response to Pearl Harbor (WWII) that no terrorist group would dream of attacking the USA. I even remember him saying, "Just let 'em try!"

September 11th, 2001 proved that we had a false sense of security!

Many people have that same false sense of security when it comes to their spiritual life. They think they can sin, they can worship any old way, they can neglect their souls and nothing is going to happen. But the Bible paints a much different picture.

Jesus spoke to this very thing. He was once speaking about the judgment and the fate of those who lived with a false sense of spiritual security. He said,

"Not everyone who says to me, 'Lord, Lord," will enter the kingdom of heaven, but the one who does the will of my Father who is in heaven.

On that day many will say to me, 'Lord, Lord, did we not prophesy in your name, and cast out demons in your name, and do mighty works in your name?' And then I will declare to them, 'I never knew you; depart from me, you workers of lawlessness." Matthew 7. 21-23

You need to make sure that the Day of the Lord will be your redemption, and not your condemnation.

You do this by being truly born again and living righteously as you await that Day.

The second danger Amos exposes is:

The Danger of Impure Worship.

Verses 21-23, 25-27

To say the least, God was not pleased with Israel's impure worship. They were worshipping idols and committing immoral acts, while at the same time giving God superficial worship.

Amos provides details and resons for God's disgust of Israel's worship.

a. Heartless worship. Verses 21-23

This graphic imagery really needs no comment. Any act of worship the Israelites engage in is unacceptable to God.

1. The feasts turn the Lord's stomach.

God says He hates, and then He uses an even stronger word for disgust, He *despises* the Israelite's feasts. These were the feasts mandated by the Mosaic Law.   Israel made God sick because they only observed them out of habit. They also probably mixed their idolatry in with the holy days.

2. The solemn assemblies stink.

God does not delight in their services and assemblies.

3. The sacrifices and offerings are ignored by God.

No matter how extravagant, no matter how grand a sacrifice, any act of worship that comes from an impure heart, and with the wrong motivations doesn't garner God's acceptance.

4. The singing and music hurt the Lord's ears.

Doesn't this show how important truth is in worship? What does this do to some of our modern "worship programs"? Beautiful music, great singing, and "meaningful songs" do not delight God unless they are done for Him and Him only.

O, church, let's never fall into entertainment. Let's worship to please and adore God...let's get out hearts in the right place before we even consider the first hymn.

Shouldn't confession be a LARGE factor in our worship?

Now bypass verse 24 for now. And pick up:

Verses 25-27

These verses prove difficult to reconcile and interpreters disagree on how they should read.   When this happens it is important to take the most literal translation, even if it isn't entirely clear what it means. Remember in the original text there were no verses so 25 and 26 would be viewed as a single unit of thought. Therefore, the best translation would be something such as,

"Did you offer sacrifices and grain offerings to Me 40

CHAPTER 11: THE DANGER OF TAINTED WORSHIP AM...   117

years in the wilderness? House of Israel, while you were taking up Sakkuth your king?" (HCSB)

The Israelites were notorious for idolatry during the Exodus. God reminds their offspring they are just like their ancestors.

Sakkun and Kaiwan were both "astral deities" of Egyptian, or Canaanite origin. They are normally thought to be representative of the planet Saturn. This makes God's proclamation in verse 8 even more ominous. He created the very planet that the people have perverted to represent a false god.

The Lord declares that Israel will fall and be removed from the Promised Land. They will be taken into exile-"beyond Damascus", far from their beloved country.

You may ask what in the world were they doing that made God so angry? Well we already know that they were immoral, idolatrous, abusive to the poor and unjust in their dealings.

Let's return to 2 Kings 17 for a minute:

...They went after false idols and became false, and they followed the nations around them, concerning whom the Lord has commanded them that they should not do like them. And they abandoned all the commandments of the Lord their God, and made for themselves metal images of two calves, and they made an Asherah and worshipped all the hosts of heaven and served Baal.

And they burned their sons and daughters as offerings and used divination and omens and sold themselves to do evil in the sight of the Lord, provoking him to anger. (15b.-17)

Yeah, I think God was justified in His wrath!

Jesus said,

"But the hour is coming, and is now here, when true worshippers will worship the Father in spirit and truth, for the

Father is seeking such people to worship him. God is spirit, and those who worship him must worship in spirit and truth." John 4. 23-24

The point being?

God is much more concerned about your heart and your righteousness than He is about your acts of worship. When you are serious about your personal holiness, when your burning desire is to please God, then your worship will be as it should. When you hate the things God hates and love the things God loves-then your worship will be pleasing to the Lord.

Fortunately, Amos tells us how to purify our tainted worship. God gives us:

The Command to Right Attitude and Action.

Verse 24

If Israel is to regain God's favor, if their worship is to ever be acceptable to him, then two things need to happen.

1. Justice must "roll down like waters".

The metaphor is easy to understand. Justice, treating others fairly, and according to Scripture, must flow freely.

They should treat everyone fairly and show no favoritism toward the "higher" classes. They need to take seriously the mandate to look after widows and orphans, the hopeless, and the helpless.

2. Righteousness must roll "like an ever-flowing" stream.

Moral purity, righteous and holy acts must never "dry up". You cannot afford to let yourself fall into sin.

This requires constant diligence, prayer and repentance. When justice and righteousness flow, worship flows as well.

We find this principle at work from the very beginning

of civilization. Remember the sons of Adam and Eve, Cain and Able? Moses tells us that Cain and Abel both brought offerings (an act of worship) to the Lord. The Lord was pleased with Abel's offering and accepted it. But, God "had no regard for Cain's offering". Why not? Because Cain had an unjust and unrighteous heart. When God rejected his offering, Cain became angry. Genesis 4, 6-8 tells us what happened:

The Lord said to Cain, "Why are you angry, and why has your face fallen? If you do well, will you not be accepted? And if you do not do well, sin is crouching at the door. Its desire is for you, but you must rule over it."

(Cain's true heart is revealed in what happened next)

Cain spoke to Abel his brother. And when they were in the field, Cain rose up against his brother Abel and killed him.

It's the heart, man! It's the heart.

The prophet Micah wrote,

"He has told you, o man, what is good; and what does the Lord require of you but to do justice, and to love kindness, and walk humbly with your God?" Micah 6.8

Treating others fairly and living morally pure lives should be the "ebb and flow" of the everyday life of believers.

We must avoid the danger of false security. The danger of tainted worship is God's judgment.

We must obey God's command to do justice and live righteously. Then we can be assured that God will be pleased and accept our worship.

Have you ever had food poisoning? It's a pleasant experience isn't it? Food poisoning is a strange thing. You eat some tainted food and you get sick. You'd think if you avoided tainted food you wouldn't get sick. Easy to avoid, right? The problem is tainted food can be deceptive. You cannot see the bacteria that ruin the food. It usually looks ok. It usually smells ok. It usually tastes ok. It usually fills you up and satisfies you. But after a few hours, man do you get sick. If you had been able to look at the food under a microscope you would have seen the bacteria, and not eaten the food.

That's how insidious tainted worship can be. It usually looks ok. People sing, praise, testify and give. Yet, the hidden things, the sin, the unrighteousness, the injustice, taints it to the point of being rotten. We need to look at ourselves under the microscope of God's Word. We need to make sure our lives are free from the "bacteria" of sin. Therefore our worship will be pleasing to God.

This begins by making sure that Christ has forgiven your sin and is the Lord of your life. If He isn't then it's time to welcome Him to be.

CHAPTER 12:
THE DANGER OF COMPLACENCY
AMOS 6. 1-3

Twin brothers, Alex and Brett Harris founded a movement called Rebelution. They described this movement's philosophy as "a teenage rebellion against low expectations". In an article about the dangers of complacency (another word for low expectations) they wrote,

Complacency is a blight that saps energy, dulls attitudes, and causes a drain in the brain. The first symptom is satisfaction with things as they are. The second is rejection of things as they might be. "Good enough" becomes today's watchword and tomorrow's standard. [1]

The Israelites, in the time of Amos had certainly grown complacent. They were living in a period of peace and prosperity. God had subdued their enemies. They were living in their own land.

They were a "mighty" and influential nation. They were experiencing economic growth.

You would think they would be grateful for God's blessing. You would think that they were living holy lives that pleased Him. Unfortunately, this was far from the case.

Because they were complacent, all sorts of sin had crept into their lives. Greed, immorality, idolatry, injustice, and many other sins were spawned by their complacent attitudes.

Just what is complacency anyway? The dictionary defines complacency, or complacent as:" quiet satisfaction, contentment, self-satisfaction or "smugness". Synonyms for complacency include, arrogant, self-righteous, unconcerned, proud, satisfied or smug.

Israel had fallen in love with herself, and out of love with God. They were happy with the status quo and didn't see any need to change it. God saw it otherwise. He warned them of impending judgment if they didn't repent, and start living by His commands. Unfortunately, history tells us they didn't get the message.

The teaching of this passage is that we must never fall into complacent living. We must never accept what is unacceptable to God. We should be constantly growing and maturing in our faith. To just be happy with the way things are (when there is always something to improve) breaks the very heart of God. Complacency also stifles His ongoing work of sanctification in our lives.

This passage gives a complete treatment to the problem of complacency. Amos states his proposition; he then illustrates, and applies it.

His goal is to bring the nation back to the Lord before judgment comes. His instrument of judgment wouls be in the form of the Assyrian army.

Amos' proposition is:

The Danger of Careless Living. Verse 1

Generically this type of oracle is called a "woe oracle" (see the opening word, hoy, "Woe") and develops from the laments connected to funerals. However, its prophetic use doesn't relate to an actual death; rather, it communicates that the addressee is "as good as dead".[2]

Hoy "woe" is an interjection meaning ho! Woe! Alas! It is used in lamenting a person's death (I Kings 13.30). It is used in prophetic announcements of judgment or threats (Isa 1.4; 24, Jer 48.1; Ezek 13.18, Amos 5.18). It is used to draw attention to an unexpected but momentous occasion (Isa 18.1) ...[3] It is a cry of anguish and pain.

Amos "preaches the funeral" of those at ease in Zion. To be at ease (sa'anan) basically means to be complacent, or free from care, or worries because of being in a privileged class of people. Secondarily it is the resultant arrogant attitude that comes from being complacent. The Israelites had become complacent because of their status as God's chosen people.

They thought they could go on worshipping idols, exploiting the poor, engaging in gross immorality, having drunken parties, offering God tainted worship, and so forth with impunity.

They had become arrogant and sinful because they thought that nothing, or no one could touch them. They were very wrong. They were living carelessly, even recklessly.

Amos calls them out! This unsophisticated farmer from the backwoods of Tekoa looks the rich, powerful political and religious "movers and shakers" in the eye and says, "You think you are blessed, untouchable: but you are really dead men!"

Jesus gave us a great illustration of this kind of careless, complacent living in the parable of the rich fool. Luke chapter 12 records this parable,

And He told them a parable, saying, "The land of a rich man produced plentifully, and he thought to himself, "What shall I do, for I have nowhere to store my crops?" And he said, "I will do this: I will tear down my barns and build larger ones, and there I will store my grain and my goods. And I will say to my soul, "Soul, you have ample goods laid up for many years; relax, eat, drink, be merry."'

But God said to him, "Fool! This night your soul is required of you, and the things you have prepared, whose will they be?" So is the one who lays up treasure for himself and is not rich toward God. (16-21)

What is the "moral of this story?"

No nation, individual, or church can afford thoughtless living, no matter how strong, wealthy or "blessed" they may be. Complacency leads to pride, other sins and laziness, which will ultimately lead to judgment.

Listen to the words of the wise one:

"Toward the scorners he is scornful, but to the humble he gives favor." Proverbs 3.34

The proposition is obvious. Easy living will bring about destruction. Amos illustrates this fact from recent events of his day. He next gives us:

The Example of Fallen Nations. Verse 2

God uses the examples of some great cities that fell to let Israel know they are not exempt from His judgment.

(1) Calneh was in Syria. It had been destroyed by the Assyrian army some 200 years prior to Amos' ministry. Its demise would have been well known to Israel.

(2) Hamath was also a Syrian city that had been conquered by the current King of Israel Jeroboam II. This happened during Amos' ministry and was therefore very much a current event (Cf. 2 Kings 14.28).

(3) Gath was a city in Philistia and had been recently conquered by King Uzziah the king of Judah (Cf. 2 Chronicles 26.6). This was another reference to current events.

The interesting thing about these cities is that they were all stronger than any of the cities in Israel, including Samaria, the current capital. Amos asks two penetrating questions: Is Israel any better than these cities? It's an indictment, no they aren't: they are morally and socially corrupt. Is Israel any bigger than these cities-meaning are they any mightier in number or resources? The answer of course is, "No". The fall of these cities ought to serve as a warning to Samaria. No city or nation is too mighty to fall.

This has historically been the attitude of many of the great cities or nations that have fallen throughout history. Think of Japan, Germany, and the UK. Recently, Tunisia, Egypt, Iceland, Ireland, Greece, Ukraine, the Sudan, and Libya: is the USA next?

The fall of the "great ones" should serve as a reminder that no nation, no person, no community, no church , no matter how big, wealthy, or powerful can afford to become complacent.

There was once a time when the Southern Baptist denomination was the strongest evangelical Christian denomination on the planet. We baptized more people, sent out more missionaries, built more schools, and started more churches and ministries than any other Christian group on the planet. That is simply not true today. According to our research arm, Lifeway Resources, our membership declined by over 100,000 members in 2013. Our baptism rates are the lowest on record since 1948. Fewer and fewer men are submitting to pastoral ministry and missions.

There was a time when Southern Baptists had a strong voice in the culture and exerted a great deal of influence in society: this simply isn't true today! It's predicted that if these trends aren't arrested there won't be much left of the SBC by the year 2050.

Why? The main reason is that we became complacent. We became enamored with ourselves, our size, our

money, our politics, some of our "stars" and we left Jesus out...
and now we are paying for it!

The SBC, if we don't wake up and get our priorities
straight, is going to go the way of the mainline denominations
and wither and eventually die.

Complacency is extremely dangerous. Learn from
the examples of others and don't fall into it.

How many "great" nations have risen and fell over the
centuries? How many rich, famous, and powerful people have
come to ruin? How many once great churches are now empty
and abandoned? Complacency and the problems it causes has
humbled many of the mighty.

Paul warned the Corinthians:

"Therefore let anyone who thinks that he stands take
heed lest he fall." I Corinthians 10.12

Amos has explained his proposition; he has illustrated
that proposition, now he applies that proposition. He shows us,

The Need to Live in Reality. Verse 3

The complacent Israelites won't even think about being
subdued by an enemy. They are so far gone that the threat
doesn't even alarm them. The day is far away, let's eat, drink and
be merry.

They "bring near the seat of violence" in the sense
that they continue to oppress the poor, creating a "reign of
violence" against their own countrymen.

They needed to wake up. They needed to heed the
reality check Amos is giving them. But they don't, and they
won't, and they will be conquered, and exiled. They should have
been on their faces repenting, but instead, they carried right
along as if they had all the time in the world.

Once again, Jesus told a parable that illustrates this point so well. Pull out your Bible and find Matthew chapter 25 and locate verse 14. Here in the well-known parable of the talents we find a great illustration of someone who needed to face reality, but refused to do so.

For it will be like a man going on a journey, who called his servants and entrusted to them his property. To one he gave five talents, to another two, to another one, to each according to his ability. Then he went away.

He who had received the five talents went at once and traded with them, and he made five talents more.

So also he who had the two talents made two talents more.

But he who had received the one talent went and dug in the ground and hid his master's money.

Now after a long time the master of those servants came and settled accounts with them.

And he who had received the five talents came forward, bringing five talents more, saying, 'Master, you delivered to me five talents; here I have made five talents more.'

His master said to him, 'Well done, good and fathful servant. You have been faithful over a little; I will set you over much. Enter into the joy of your master."

And he also who had the two talents came forward, saying, "Master, you delivered to me two talents; here I have mafe two talents more."

His master said to him, "Well done, good and faithful servant. You have been faithful over a little; I will set you over much. Enter into the joy of your master."

He also who had received the one talent came forward, saying, 'Master, I knew you to be a hard man, reaping where you did not sow, and gathering where you scattered no seed, so I was afraid, and I went and hid your talent in the ground. Here you have what is yours."

But his his master answered him, "You wicked and slothful servant! You knew that I reap where I have not sown and gathered where I scattered no seed? Then you ough to have invested my money with the bankers, and at my coming I should have received what was my own with interest.

So take the talent from him and give it to him who has the ten talents.

For everyone who has will more be given, and he will have an abundance. But from the one who has not, even what he has will be taken away.

And cast the worthless servant into the outer darkness. In that place there will be weeping and gnashing of teeth.

It is the height of foolishness to think that God will withhold His judgment forever. You cannot afford to be blind to events unfolding in the world and in your life. It's an old saying, but a true saying, "You better live like it's your last day on earth because it may very well be."

(Jesus said) "Therefore, stay awake, for you do not know which day your Lord is coming." Matthew 24.42

Complacency, as we have seen is deadly, God's people should be diligent to avoid it.

Some self-examination is in order here, isn't it? Have you become complacent? Here are nine signs that you fallen into complacency:

1. You are careless with your moral life.

2. You aren't looking up for the return of Jesus Christ.

3. Your devotional habits are lacking.

4. You no longer witness to others.

5. You see the denigration of our culture, our society, and our faith and you just try to hang on instead of working to redeem it.

6. You are every happy with the way things ARE and see no need to improve or change anything.

7. You spend more time thinking about the way things used to be than how they should be now.

8. You look at other fallen people, churches and nations and think, 'That could never happen to me, or to us."

9. You truly can get along just fine without the Lord.

There is only one cure for complacency and that is the Lord Jesus Christ. In Him, we find the cure, and the motivation to stay red hot in our pursuit of God, and His holiness.

[1] http://www.goodreads.com/quotes/tag/complacency

[2] Longman and Garland, 402

[3] Zodhiates, 1944

CHAPTER 13: THE DANGER OF SELF-INDULGENCE AMOS 6. 4-7

The morning of December 7th, 1941 is called the "Day of Infamy". This is the day that the Japanese bombed Pearl Harbor resulting in the loss of 2300 American lives. It also thrust the US into the Second World War, which they had been reluctant to enter up until that point. This seemed like a sneak attack that came without warning. However, over the years the truth has been uncovered. The truth is that there had been repeated warnings that the Japanese planned to bomb Pearl Harbor. For over a year prior to the attack, reliable sources had warned US intelligence that the Japanese had plans to bomb Pearl Harbor, and they needed to be prepared...but we were not...and it costed us dearly. It's as if no cared, or were too busy enjoying life to take notice. The whole world was at war...you would have thought the US would have taken the threats seriously...but they didn't...

A similar scenario was being played out in Israel about 2800 years earlier. Israel had fallen into sin and God was planning to send judgment upon them. This judgment would come in the form of the Assyrian Army that would conquer and destroy the nation. Those that didn't die in the attack would be carried off as exiles to Assyria. God sent the prophets to warn Israel, to lead the nation to repentance, but they were ignored. They were so deep into sin, and so self-indulgent that they didn't take the warnings seriously: and they would seriously pay for it.

Friends, we live in a time of unprecedented self-indulgence. If we don't repent and return to moderate, sober, and conscious living, then we too can expect God to send judgment upon us.

In preaching against Israel's self-indulgence, Amos gives us two main thoughts to consider. First,

The Description of Self-Indulgence. Verses 4-6

Amos continues pronouncing "woes" upon Israel. Recall the Hebrew word translated "woe" conveys the idea of great distress, gloom and death. He is basically pronouncing a death sentence for the nation. He has already pronounced woe upon them because of their tainted worship and their complacency. Now he shifts to condemning their sinful self-indulgence.

Let's walk through these verses and see what they were doing that made God so angry.

We find Israel indulging in sins of commission (things they were doing), as well as sins of omission (things they were supposed to be doing but weren't). First let's look at their:

Sins of Commission:

1. Laziness, lethargy, luxury, idleness, apathy.

The condemnation was for those who lie on beds of ivory and stretch themselves out on their couches. Whether Amos is speaking of a literal bed made out of ivory (which even in those days would have been excessive luxury), or speaking figuratively of Israel's excessive self-indulgence in extravagant pleasures, really doesn't matter. The point is clear: they spent way too much money and cared too much about luxuries. Recall now that one of the main sins of Israel at the time was their greed and dishonesty. Many had gotten rich by exploiting the poor. This makes the image all the more revolting.

An even greater offense to God was their general demeanor. They were lying about; sprawling on couches and beds. They had become lazy and idle, apathetic to what was going on around them. Stretching out also carries the idea of riotous, carefree revelry. They were partying, lying around getting drunk, indulging themselves when they should have been serving the Lord.

2. Gluttony.

They also ate lambs from the flock and calves from the midst of the stall. Here again, we find Israel going for the rich delicacies, and indulging themselves. Lambs and calves were rarely eaten except on special occasions (the prodigal son's family killed the "fatted calf" on his return). Yet, the Israelites were gorging themselves on the most expensive and fine cuisine. They were doing this while many in their country were starving.

The idea of overindulgence, outright gluttony is implied here as well. It calls to mind Jesus' parable of the rich man and Lazarus. The rich man ate the finest foods; he had more than enough, while poor Lazarus begged for a few crumbs of bread...which he never got! By the way, look up that parable, and see how that story ended.

We see this in our nation today. Saint and sinner alike eat way too much, way too often, and way too extravagantly. When compared with other nations, our portion sizes are 25-50% bigger. In my town, you can drive down the street on your way to the Golden Corral and pass homeless people who haven't eaten all day and homes occupied by underfed children and elderly people.   I'll bet your town is no different. That's certainly something to soul search about, isn't it?

3. Excessive, bawdy and irreverent entertainment.

They sing idle songs to the sound of the harp.   An idle song refers to a song that is composed on the spot; it is an improvised song usually sang in a vain and self-centered manner.   These songs were irreverent and usually of a bawdy nature. This is made even worse because they thought they were like David in the sense they thought their drunken, irreverent and bawdy songs were somehow pleasing to the ear, or even acceptable to God like the Psalms of David were. The implication here is one of an entertainment oriented society that has lost all sense of decency, and nothing is off limits in the name of entertainment. Does that sound like any nation you know of?

Have you noticed how obsessed with entertainment we have become?   According to the Nielsen company who does research on American television viewing habits, the average American over the age of 2 watches television an average of 34 hours per week! 34 hours per week! That's almost a full-time job.[1]

It's also estimated that Americans spend 23 hours per week online and texting.[2] Combine the two and you get 57 hours a week spend mainly on entertainment!

You and I both know that most of our entertainment doesn't pass the test of being acceptable to God. Bathroom humor, and sexual innuendoes dominate "comedy".

Murder and violence pass for "action".

Illicit sex accounts for most "romance" and drama"...it's all trash. What if the average American spent 57 hours per week reading the Bible, or witnessing, or serving in the church? My God!

4. Drunkenness.

They drank their wine in bowls. Goblets and cups were no longer sufficient. They swilled their wine by the bowlful! Excess, drunkenness, debauchery was the order of the day... truthfully it still is today.

5. Vain and opulent self-love.

They anoint themselves with the finest oils. They extravagantly cared for their own bodies. Oils, lotions, perfumes, cosmetics were all used in the ancient world by men and women, just like today, to beautify themselves. Some of these could be quite expensive. Remember when Mary used her "nard" on the feet of Christ? The price of that lotion was an average year's wages.

The Israelites lavished themselves. They pampered themselves with the finest beauty products and "toiletries" they could find. How many thousands of dollars do American Christians spend each year on self-indulgent "beauty" products? Face creams, make-up, special soaps, and the like? Guys quit looking at the ladies; you are just as bad or worse!

The most expensive men's cologne in the world is Clive Christian (ironic, huh?) no. 1 Perfume for Men. Listen to how it is described:

This is the most expensive bottle of men's perfume in the world.

Aside from being made from some of the rarest ingredients that are harvested from different parts of the world, it is packaged in a bottle made from crystal and its neck is made of gold. If that isn't luxurious enough, then it should be known that there is a five karat diamond included in the gold inset. Originating from the late 1800's, its stopper is designed just like the original pattern which was granted by her majesty herself, Queen Victoria. This perfume not only makes a man smell terrific, it makes him feel royal, too.

How much does it cost? Only $2,350 an ounce! My first two cars didn't cost that much! For that price it better wash my car and mow my grass! Trust me; there are people who will buy it...

Pastor and theologian Dietrich Bonhoeffer who was executed by the Nazis had this to say about the sin of self-indulgence:

"The real difference in the believer who follows Christ and has mortified his will and died after the old man in Christ, is that he is more clearly aware than other men of the rebelliousness and perennial pride of the flesh, he is conscious of his sloth and self-indulgence and knows that his arrogance must be eradicated. Hence there is a need for daily self-discipline."

— Dietrich Bonhoeffer, The Cost of Discipleship[3]

We have seen what Israel was doing that angered God. Now let's think about what they were *not* doing that grieved the Lord. Look at the last part of verse 6:

B. Sins of Omission:

But are not grieved over the ruin of Joseph.

To be grieved means to be sick, to be distressed, weak and sorrowful. They should have been heartsick and repentant knowing that ruin (judgment and destruction was coming), but they weren't. They were too busy having fun, partying, and pampering themselves to care. Four issues are implied here. They were:

1. Not sick over the state of affairs.

They should have been on their faces, repenting, sorry for their sin, begging God for His mercy. They should have looked out at the immorality, the idolatry, the violence, and been soul sick: but there weren't.

2. Oblivious to prophetic warnings.

Amos warned them, Hosea warned them, Isaiah and Jeremiah warned them, Zephaniah, Zechariah, Haggai, they all warned them of pending judgment, but they would not listen!

They were in sad state of moral and spiritual failure:

3. Failure to obey the most basic of commandments.

God wasn't enforcing some debatable fine point of theology with Israel. It was the basic things, such as avoiding idols, and immorality and treating others with dignity and respect that they were failing to do.

4. Failure to use wealth and influence for the good of others.

There is no doubt that God had blessed His people with wealth, with peace, with influence...which they were supposed to use to lead the pagan nations to worship the one true God... but they didn't!

Isaiah paints a very clear picture of the self-indulgent, sinful state of the southern kingdom. The conditions of the north were identical:

Woe to those who rise early in the morning, that they may run after strong drink, as wine inflames them! They have lyre and harp, tambourine and flute and wine at their feasts, but they do not regard the deeds of the Lord, or see the work of His hands...Woe to those who call evil good and good evil, who put darkness for light and light for darkness, who put bitter for sweet and sweet for bitter!

Woe to those who are wise in their own eyes, and shrewd in their own sight! Woe to those who are heroes at drinking wine, and valiant men in mixing strong drink, who acquit the guilty for a bribe, and deprive the innocent of his right! Isaiah 5. 11-12; 20-23

So, dear reader, listen to me! Be careful that you not become self-indulgent, extravagant consumers, and neglect to love, obey and serve the Lord!

God will not allow people to live in self-indulgent luxury and ignore Him forever. In verse 7 Amos speaks of:

The Demise of the Self-Indulgent. Verse 7

Here are two eternal truths concerning those who are wicked and self-indulgent. If you tend to be a self-indulgent person you might want to take notice:

a. **The self-indulgent revelers will be the first to fall!**

They shall be the first of those who go into exile. The rich, pampered, greedy, self-indulgent of Israel will be the first to fall! To be exiled, removed from the Promised Land. and carried off to a pagan land was the worst possible thing a Hebrew could imagine. They would lose their status, their fortunes (remember others will live in their homes and drink their wine).

Do you see the word picture Amos is drawing? The self-indulgent are laying around on their ivory couches, eating fine foods, drinking bowls of wine, oblivious to the suffering around them. They sing their stupid songs, they laugh at their stupid jokes, while ignoring the immorality and injustice around them. When all of a sudden the barbarian hoard bursts in, kills a few of them and kidnaps the rest! They will be reduced to slave status.

Secondly,

b. The "party" will come to an abrupt end.

Their revelry shall pass away. Revelry refers to wild drunken, out of control parties. It also carries the idea of opulent feasting or "banqueting".

Picture the infield on Derby Day and you get the idea. This will abruptly come to a halt as God executes his judgment on them.

A modern illustration of this would be the rise and fall of Jim and Tammy Faye Bakker and their PTL and Heritage USA Empire. At one time they were super wealthy , famous, and there seemed to be no end. Yet, scandal rocked them. Before long it was discovered they had engaged in opulent living that made some Saudi Sheiks look like street people. Their lives were filled with excess after excess, immorality after immorality... all gained at the expense of trusting souls. When they fell, they fell hard. This is exactly what happened to Israel and it can happen to an individual, a church, or a nation that becomes self-indulgent. Be very careful.

James speaks of this principle in his epistle,

Come now, you rich, weep and howl for the miseries that are coming upon you. Your riches have rotted and your garments are moth eaten. Your gold and silver have corroded, and their corrosion will be evidence against you and will eat your flesh like fire. You have laid up treasure in the last days. Behold, the wages of the laborers who mowed your fields, which you kept back by fraud, are crying out against you, and the cries of the harvesters have reached the ears of the Lord of hosts.

You have lived in luxury and in self-indulgence. You have fattened your hearts in a day of slaughter. You have condemned and murdered the righteous person. He does not resist you. James 5. 1-6

Reckless excess and wanton self-indulgence leads only to ruin.

Please don't misunderstand what this passage is teaching. God wants us to be joyful. He doesn't mind our celebrating, or enjoying tasty foods, or engaging in "clean" entertainment. But, it's when we do these things to excess, when we neglect the important things in life, when we cast Him aside to pursue them...that's when we have a problem.

We aren't called to stoic, Spartan living...though it wouldn't hurt us...but we are called to be sensible, frugal and prudent. We are called to "examine ourselves". We are called to be moderate and sober in all things. We are called to care for the needy and hurting. Will you take some time and take a hard look at your life? Are you an excessive person? Do you have to have the finest of things? Do you have to eat the best foods? Are you lazy and idle? Are you so wrapped up in entertainment that you don't even care about the lost and dying world you live in?

Only Jesus Christ can give you the desire to break free of the sin of self-indulgence. Do you know Him?

1]   http://www.nydailynews.com/entertainment/tv-movies/americans-spend-34-hours-week-watching-tv-nielsen-numbers-article-1.1162285

[2] http://news.yahoo.com/americans-spend-23-hours-per-week-online-texting-092010569.html

[3]   http://www.goodreads.com/quotes/tag/self-indulgence

CHAPTER 14: THE DANGER OF PRIDE
AMOS 6. 8-14

When I was younger I was given a copy of a poem written by Willian Ernest Henley entitled: *Invictus* (which is Latin for unconquerable). At the time I read it, I thought it sounded really good and taught a mindset that was worth adopting. Listen to this:

Out of the night that covers me,

Black as the Pit from pole to pole,

I thank whatever gods may be

For my unconquerable soul.

In the fell clutch of circumstance

I have not winced nor cried aloud.

Under the bludgeonings of chance

My head is bloody, but unbowed.

Beyond this place of wrath and tears

Looms but the Horror of the shade,

And yet the menace of the years

Finds, and shall find, me unafraid.

It matters not how strait the gate,

How charged with punishments the scroll.

I am the master of my fate:

I am the captain of my soul.

William Ernest Henley

I'm ashamed to admit that for years I lived out the philosophy of this poem. The problem was I was having trouble holding up my bloodied head and mastering my fate and "captaining" my own soul. Realizing I could not handle my own life drove me to Christ.

Many years later, I was in a church service and the pastor read that poem. I thought hey, I know this one; this is going to be good! Then he went on to blast it for its arrogant denial of God's sovereignty and Lordship. That was a real turning point for me that day. My pastor who wasn't normally a "prophetic" preacher spoke prophetically to me that day ,and truthfully that message changed the course of my life.

In this passage, Amos is a prophetic in the truest sense of the word. He is speaking divine truth to Israel in an attempt to change the course of their lives.

The individual and corporate lives of Israel were marked by severe apostasy. They had abandoned God; and fallen into idolatry, immorality and every self-indulgent sin under the sun. They had become proud and arrogant. These are two sins that that God particularly despises. He was getting ready to judge them, and this was their wake up call. A call which they didn't heed!

Ah, the cry the humanist! Our bloodied and unbowed heads are proof that we indeed are not the masters of our own fate. The "Pit" will prove to many misguided fools that they were indeed not the masters of their own fates, nor the captains of their own souls.

The teaching of this passage is very clear: pride is dangerous! Pride always precedes a fall, and the fall tends to be very great!\ This warning about the danger of pride can be divided into three general thoughts. First,

God's Attitude Toward Pride and Self-Assurance. Verse 8.a.-b.

God swears by Himself, for there is none greater. He makes an oath on His character, His truth, His power, His justice and His holiness. He minces no words:

1. He abhors Israel's pride.

To "abhor" something means to utterly detest it. This is the only time this particular word is used in the whole Bible. It means to detest, to shudder, and shrink away in disgust. God hates pride, especially pride among His people. They thought they were untouchable because of their status as God's chosen people.

Also,

2. He hates Israel's strongholds.

This is an indication that God is so disgusted with Israel and its sin that He has no regard for its defense. He will not protect the nation from the invaders that He is sending as judgment. Israel was self-assured. They had a mighty army, they were prosperous, they were well defended...yet they had forgotten their God.

So, you can summarize God's attitude toward pride and self-assurance simply by saying, "HE HATES IT!"

The Bible is full of stories of men and women whose pride got them into trouble with God. King Nebuchadnezzar is a good example. After he witnessed the events in the fiery furnace he feared God. But as time went on he fell back into sinful ways. Daniel (of lion's den fame) warned him to repent and turn to the Lord, but he didn't see the need. Let's pick up the story in Daniel 4. 28-33:

All this came upon King Nebuchadnezzar. At the end of twelve months he was walking on the roof of the royal palace in Babylon, and the king answered and said, "Is not this great Babylon, which I have built by my mighty power as a royal residence and for the glory of my majesty?" While the words were still in the king's mouth, there fell a voice from heaven, "O King Nebuchadnezzar, to you it is spoken: the kingdom has departed from you, and you shall be driven from among men, and your dwelling shall be with the beasts of the field.

And you shall be made to eat grass like an ox, and seven periods of time shall pass over you, until you know that the Most High rules the kingdom of men and gives it to whom he will." Immediately the word was fulfilled against Nebuchadnezzar. He was driven from among men and ate grass like an ox, and his body was wet with the dew of heaven till his hair grew as long as eagle's feathers, and his nails were like bird's claws.

God hates pride and self-reliance. The arrogant see no need for God. They blindly follow their own whims and create themselves in "their own image".

We must be wary of:

1. Personal pride and self-reliance.

2. National pride.

3. Religious pride.

We must live in desperate dependence on God and acknowledge His lordship in all our affairs.

Solomon wrote,

"Everyone who is arrogant in heart is an abomination to the Lord; be assured, he will not go unpunished." Proverbs 16.5

Let's move on to to verses 12-13 now so that we can get a very clear picture of:

The Attributes of the Proud and Self-Assured.
Verse 12-13

Here we find four attributes of the proud and self-assured.

1. They just don't live in reality.

Notice the metaphorical language Amos uses to describe the distorted realty of the proud. Do horses run on rocks? Well, no. If they do, they will trip and break their legs. Yet, the sinful proud and self-assured run headlong into sin and corruption without so much as a second thought.

Does one plow there with oxen? You can't cultivate rocks. Yet, the people tried to cultivate their spiritual lives by engaging in idolatry-it was absurd, it just wouldn't happen. But proud, self-assured people often don't have a firm grasp of reality.

Bucky O'Neil of Arizona was one of those legendary western figures that have been embellished into the American mythology often associated with men of the "wild west". He was an Indian fighter, a lawman, gunfighter and soldier of the first rank. He was a very intelligent man. He was also a very arrogant man. He joined Theodore Roosevelt's "Rough-Riders" and was one of the top commanders. During the liberation of Cuba, during a very intense firefight He was standing tall and proud while his men were hunkered down in a trench. One of his men said, "Captain, you need to get out of the line of fire." O'Neil looked at him and said, "The Spanish bullet is not molded that will kill me".

A few seconds later a sniper proved the absurdity of that statement. Bucky died with a bullet to the head!

2. The Proud and Self-Assured pervert what is good and turn it into evil.

They have turned sweet justice into poison. Holy righteousness into bitter wormwood.

They have so perverted justice, the court system, and the civil authority, that instead of protecting people's rights and lives, they are killing them like poison. Justice is supposed to be sweet, but they have twisted and manipulated and exploited justice to the point that has become bitter.

3. They rejoice in accomplishments that really amount to nothing.

You who rejoice in Lo-debar...The Hebrew word "Lo-debar" literally means nothing. This was an Aramean region that Israel had recently conquered. They were taking credit for the victory; they didn't give God the glory. They boasted and bragged, yet in God's eyes they hadn't accomplished much at all.

Even worse:

4. They take credit for victories when the credit belongs to the Lord.

Have we not in our own strength captured Karnaim for ourselves?

Karnaim was the location of another recent military victory.

They should have given God the praise and credit for the victory, but they were too proud and self-assured to admit they were helpless without Him.

This is one of the proud and self-assured's worst offenses...not giving God the credit and glory for all things.

It would be wise to examine your own life to make

sure you aren't displaying any of the attributes of the proud and self-assured.

The prideful and self-assured distort reality and turn things that are good into things that are evil. In God's eyes, all our attempts at prideful achievement and self-aggrandizement are nothing. The grandest human achievement in any field be it arts, science, finance, architecture, or sports cannot compare to the works of the Lord. It is a sign of spiritual maturity when you accept the fact that you live, survive, and thrive by God's grace.

The wise in wrote,

"Before destruction a man's heart is haughty, but humility comes before honor." Proverbs 18.12

TS: We have already established that God hates pride, and we have just seen the signs of pride. Let's now face a sobering thought as we consider,

God's Actions Against the Proud and Self-Assured. Verses 8c.-11, 14

Verses 8c.

God will deliver them up! This means He will hand them over to their enemy. He will not only abandon them to the consequences of their sin, He will personally make sure that they are conquered and humiliated and exiled! He will hand the Assyrian army the keys to the city and say, "Have at it!" I don't know about you, but that is a frightening concept to me. That ought to serve as strong motivation to avoid pride and self-assurance.

Verses 9-10

This is a very difficult paragraph to translate and interpret. Scholars offer many explanations but none are really certain. Let me give you the best interpretation in keeping with the overall context of the passage.

The meaning is obvious. There is going to be death and destruction for Israel's future. Even if there are ten men in a house or fortress, they will not survive. There might be one who escapes the conqueror by hiding deep within the house. When the close relative comes around to deal with the dead, he will yell into the home to see if there are any survivors. Should there be one they will reply.

In Hebrew the dialogue in verse 10 suggests that the "survivor" answers with a curse by using God's name in vain. Then the relative interrupts and scolds him by saying the Lord's name shouldn't even be mentioned in the wake of such tragedy. Even in a curse. The implication is that they got what they deserved!

Verse 11

This really needs little commentary. The rich and mighty will fall. Also, the poor and the not so mighty will fall as well. All those who are proud and self-assured will face God's judgment. I do want to make a brief comment here.

It is not just the rich and powerful that can be proud and self-assured. The poor and marginalized, even the oppressed, can be just as proud and just as self-assured as the rich and powerful elite: sometimes more so! Anyone, great or small that will not acknowledge their dependence on God and submit to His Lordship will face His judgment.

Verse 14

God reveals just how He is going to judge the nation. He is going to "raise up" a nation to oppress or conquer Israel. From the extreme north (Leb-Hamath) to the extreme south (Arabah) and all points in between, they will be defeated and exiled. No one will escape God's punishment for their sin.

In 2014, we commemorated the 70th anniversary of the invasion of Normandy, which we normally refer to as D-Day. We all owe a tremendous debt to those men who fought that bloody battle, many of them giving the ultimate sacrifice. This was the turning point in the European theater during WWII. The Nazi's occupied all of France and a great deal of Europe by this point. They were strong, they were arrogant. They were certainly led by a demon-possessed madman named Hitler. They thought they could not lose.

In Nazi thought they were right no matter what they did or who they did it to. But history has proven that their arrogance and self-assurance was not enough. Right prevailed at the cost of over 60 million lives. That was 2.5% of the population at that time. This is an example of a just war and not being arrogant, but we know that God was behind the Allied victory.

This illustrates the truth that no one, no matter how strong, how smart, how powerful, how wealthy, how charismatic, can live arrogantly and self-assured forever. Sooner or later (as Johnny Cash sang) "God's gonna' cut you down." You need to take a hard look at how think and how you live. Are you headed for a fall?

Sooner or later God humbles all those who are prideful and self-assured. The fall is usually "great".

This is avoidable if you live obediently, giving God all honor, praise and glory. All your confidence should be grounded in your faith and trust in the Lord.

Paul, whom the Lord used in a mighty way, knew better that to be arrogant or self-assured. He wrote,

"Not that we are sufficient in ourselves to claim anything as coming from us, but our sufficiency is from God..." 2

Corinthians 3.5

Now we know how God feels about pride and self-assurance, we know the signs and we know the results. We must adjust our lives according to these truths.

In the beginning of this chapter I told you about the poem Invictus. The man who gave me this poem truly lived by i's creed. He had no respect for anyone, including the Lord. Over the years I watched him fight needless battle after battle all because of his pride, arrogance and self-assurance. His life wound up in terrible tragedy. He lost everything, including his family. Yes, his head was unbowed, but it was bloody, so bloody.

Contrast this experience with that of King Nebuchadnezzar. After God struck him down and he basically became an animal, he writes:

At the end of the days, I, Nebuchadnezzar, lifted my eyes to heaven, and my reason returned to me, and I blessed the Most High, and praised and honored him who lives forever, for his dominion is an everlasting dominion, and his kingdom endures from generation to generation; all the inhabitants of the earth are accounted as nothing, and he does according to his will among the hosts of heaven and among the inhabitants of the earth; and none can stay his hand or say to him, "What have you done?"

At the same time my reason returned to me, and for the glory of my kingdom, my majesty and my splendor returned to me. My counselors and my lords sought me, and I was established in my kingdom, and still more greatness was added to me. Now I, Nebuchadnezzar, praise and extol and honor the King of Heaven, for all his works are right and his ways are just; and those who walk in pride he is able to humble. (Daniel 4. 34-37)

Which way would you rather go?

Let me tell you: your head better be bowed beloved! If not, God will bow it for you! Anyone who takes a prideful approach to life will eventually wind up in ruin. We are not the masters of our own destinies. We must submit to almighty God! Only in Him can we know true freedom. Only with Him as our Master can we be spared the ultimate judgment. Only by being his "slaves" can we know true freedom and peace.

We must admit we are lost and cannot save ourselves. As Christians we must admit that we cannot do anything of consequence without Him. Where do you stand with Him?

CHAPTER 15: TWO PRAYERS AND A PLUMB LINE AMOS 7. 1-9

I had a long and varied career in law-enforcement. Many of those years were spent in the Patrol Division. Let me tell you something, there is no such thing as "routine" patrol. Every day you ran into something new and interesting. I have gone on every kind of call you can imagine. Everything from robberies to haunted houses, you name it. One of the most common complaints I responded to were "loud party" calls. Every weekend there was a party somewhere in which the music, and the people, got too loud for the neighbors. The neighbors would call and complain. Then we were dispatched to deal with it.

Now there are a lot of laws that you can enforce at a loud party. Noise ordinances, disorderly conduct, things like that.

But normally, you didn't barge in like gangbusters and break up the party on the first call (though that is fun to do!). No, normally you went to the call. Talked to the people, told them to tone it down, and then left. Now, if you had to go back a second time you went a little more aggressively. You made some threats, you ran some people off...but you didn't normally take drastic actions.

However, if there was a third call, action was indeed required!

So you, and all your buddies went in, found every violation you could, broke up the party, put some people in jail. In the old days, we broke a few things, animate and inanimate, and put the party out of business.

Now, the party was definitely going full blast in Israel in Amos' time. God gave them repeated warnings to repent of their debauchery, their idolatry, pride and sloth, but they basically ignored Him. It was getting time for the warnings to stop, and the judgment to begin.

We are now entering the final section of the book of Amos. This is the "grand finale" if you will. In this passage Amos has three rather terrifying visions of God's judgment on Israel. The first two visions drive Amos to his face in intercession. He begs God not to send terrible judgment to Israel. God hears his prayers and relents. However, we see by the time God gives him the third vision of judgment, Amos realizes that Israel has gone too far, and judgment is inevitable. Amos doesn't even pray for their safety.

This is a rather frightening episode in Scripture. It teaches us something about the Lord, and about the sinful state of mankind. God gives us warning after warning, after warning. He calls us to repent, turn to Christ, or face judgment, but how many people really listen?

One of the most frightening prospects I can imagine is going too far in sin and rebellion. This can happen to people, nations, and churches. It is frightening to think of God pronouncing irrevocable judgment. But, it can happen.

As we break down this passage, we find out just how gracious and long-suffering God truly is. We also find that He has a breaking point. There is a point of no return. Israel had definitely reached it.

In the first movement of the passage we consider,

The Two Prayers. Verses 1-6

Verse 1a.

This is what the Lord God showed me…

That the Lord "showed" Amos indicates the prophetic nature of the visions. To "show" translates *ra'ah* and means to "cause to see" or reveal. Take note that Amos not only saw visions, but he heard the Lord's voice, and even conversed with Him. Therefore, we see the nature of prophetic gift or calling-seeing and hearing the Word of God. That's why it's so important that we study the prophets (even if it gets a bit tedious),we want to know what the Lord has to show us!

We find three things unfolding in these two prophetic visions. First, we see:

a. The Lord's Indignation. Verse 1b-2a.

The first judgment God plans to execute upon Israel is a judgment of locusts.

The Lord "raised up" a swarm of locusts to devour the spring or second harvest of grain. Ironically, the first crop was for use by the king and his government. It served as a kind of tax on the people. They continued to live opulently and excessively without regard for the people who were struggling.

The second cutting would be designated for consumption by the people. If the locusts devoured the crop, if famine came, they would starve. Nationwide famine is a devastating to a nation. We see this all too much in our world today.

This shows just how angry God was with Israel.

He was going to let them starve. He was going to wipe out their crops. Think of some of the images of famine you see on late night television. Have you seen the images of men and women who are walking skeletons? Children with bellies swollen from hunger? God was terribly offended by Israel's sin. His judgment would be severe.

God's indignation is also shown in the second vision. Look at verse 4

This is a judgment of fire or drought.

This disaster could have been a literal fire, like a rampant brush fire or forest fire that consumed everything in its path including drying up Israel's water sources. It could also symbolize a terrible drought that dried up all the water in Israel.

It really doesn't matter if this was a literal, or metaphorical fire-the results would be the same-devastation.

The point to make in these two judgments is clear: God has had it; He is indignant, offended and flat out furious, becuase His people had become so evil and wayward. He is going to take them out!

However, thank the Lord for the prophet! Thank God there are intercessors that will pray on behalf of others. Let's look at the next movement and call it:

b. The Prophet's Intercession.

Verses 2 and 5

Amos calls on God to forgive Israel. To grant them a pardon from the death sentence that they certainly deserved. He asks God how in the world Jacob (Israel) could withstand such withering judgment? How would they survive such terrible famine and drought? They are just too small, too weak, and too young to take it. Amos begs God to reconsider. Amos had a glimpse of the judgment of the Lord and he was so frightened by it that he begs God to relent.

We next see something of the amazing character of God. The third movement we can call:

c. The Calamity's Interruption.

That the Lord "relented" (KJV repented) causes some concern. The natural question arises, "If God is sovereign over all things, if He makes a declaration, how can our human intercession change His mind or prompt Him to act in anyway?"

This phrase also occurs in Exodus 34.14 where God was about to wipe out the entire tribe of Israel. Moses interceded and God "relented" and spared them.

What this does NOT mean is:

1. That God is not omniscient (all-knowing) and there are things in the future He does not see.

2. That God is not omnipotent (all-powerful) and there are things that are beyond His control.

3. That God had made up His mind (predetermined) what He was going to do and Amos' intercession had no real purpose or power.

So what is the best solution? Admit we don't understand all God's ways. He has perfect foreknowledge, He is sovereign, he does respond to our prayers. God has designed the world to operate according to His plans; these plans include His free creatures making free choices that have very real consequences. In the present case, God showed Amos a future disaster, Amos prayed, and God relented.

That was how God designed this scenario in history to work and it worked perfectly according to His plan.

Let's think about this for a minute. None of us are

prophets. No one today is going to see this kind of vision. But do we not have the Scriptures that tell us of the awful fate of sinners who will not turn to God? The Bible vividly describes hell. We know that in the end times God will pour out His fury on the earth and its inhabitants. Shouldn't we praying for God to hold off His judgment until more people are saved? Shouldn't we pray to God for our back slidden brothers and sisters not to be disciplined, and to give them more time to return to Him?

Amos' prophetic ministry occurred roughly 70 years before the Assyrian Army conquered and exiled the Northern kingdom. This suggests something. God was getting ready to take them out right then and there. Yet, through Amos' intercession, God spared Israel and gave them more time to repent.

I wonder how differently we would look at our prayer life if we took seriously that we may very well be instrumental in God averting disaster in people's lives.

God spoke through the prophet Joel,

"Yet even now", declares the Lord, return to Me with all your heart, with fasting and weeping, and with mourning; and rend your hearts and not your garments. Return to the Lord your God for He is gracious and merciful, slow to anger, and abounding in steadfast love; and He relents over disaster". Joel 2. 12-13

The importance of intercessory prayer cannot be overstated. Only in heaven will we know the effects our fervent prayers on behalf of others.

The third vision Amos writes about is one of the most disappointing scenes in the book. We'll simply call it:

The Plumb Line. Verses 7-9

The vision prompts twothoughts. The first is::

1. The Lord's Evaluation. Verses 7-8

a. The plumb line of God.

The term "plum line" is a very difficult term to translate from Hebrew. The best translation is "a lump of tin". Given the context, we can assume that the lump of tin was attached to a string, and used as a plumb line. A plumb line is simply a string with a weight on it that is used to check the vertical orientation (straightness) of objects like walls.

The vision is easily interpreted. God holds the plumb line, His truth, His holiness; His standards are the "plumb line" by which all people's "vertical orientation" (uprightness) is measured.

2. The Nation's Decimation.

Obviously, Israel was out of plumb. They were crooked with their sin. Therefore, God was going to demolish them. He will not "pass by them" this time. They don't get a pass on His judgment. It is inevitable.

Amos cannot argue this point with God. In the first two visions God didn't give a reason for bringing the disasters on Israel. Here, He does, and Amos just has to remain quiet as he realizes God is perfectly justified (as He always is) in bringing judgment.

Notice the particular places God singles out for judgment. The "high places" are the places of false and tainted worship-God hates this. He also singles out the "house of Jeroboam", the king and the ruling class. They should have led the people to follow God not into sin.

I have a question to ask. Do you think the Lord's people today would pass the plumb line test? Would the leaders of the church be found plumb? What about our nation? Is its "vertical relationship" true?

When I was a kid I worked on a survey crew quite a bit. This was back before the technology we have now. We used an old fashioned transit. One of the things you had to make sure of when you set the transit up was that it was perfectly vertical over the bench mark, or it will throw all of your measurements off. You used a plumb line to do this. The benchmark was a fixed, known point that had already been established by someone else. If you aren't perfectly vertical over the bench mark, then all your angles, and elevations will be off and the maps won't be accurate.

God's Word is the bench mark for our lives. We must set up perfectly vertical over it, or all of our other "measurements" are going to be off.

The Psalmist wrote:

"God is a righteous judge, and a God who feels indignation every day. If a man does not repent, God will whet His sword; He has bent and readied His bow; He has prepared for him His deadly weapons, making His arrows fiery shafts." Psalm 7. 12-13

God sets the standard of righteousness and is the perfect Evaluator of your life. Those who do not "measure up" will face His judgment and discipline. The ultimate "plum line" is your submission to the demands of the gospel of Jesus Christ. This is the "weight" that anchors the "string" by which He evaluates our lives.

This week I was told a discouraging story about one of the churches in my community. It seems thirty years ago it was a strong, vibrant, soul-winning church. But...they lost their vertical standing. They took their eyes off the Lord, they became selfish, they ran their pastor off and the church split. Now, it's just a shell, it has about 10-15 people where once they had 150 people. All because they "got out of plumb".

Beloved, this can happen to you in heartbeat. Once you fall out of love with God, once the cycle of sin starts, you can expect to God to take action.

So don't let this happen. God is gracious. He will relent from judgment-but you have to turn to Him in repentance and faith. Have you? If not, will you?

CHAPTER 16:
DON'T SHOOT
THE MESSENGER
AMOS 7. 10-17

How many of you have heard the phrase, "Don't shoot the messenger?" We understand that when we use this phrase it means when we get angry at someone for giving us some bad news or news we don't want to hear. If a person is just the "bearer of bad news" and has no personal involvement with the event then you shouldn't "shoot him" just for telling you the truth.

I was curious about the origin of this common saying, so I did a little checking. Apparently, the phrase developed from several events some of which were true and other fictitious.

One is a line from an ancient anthology of biographies called Plutarch's Lives of Noble Greeks and Romans.

It seems a certain Tigranes was involved in a battle when he received a bad report concerning his enemy, Lucullus. The line reads,

"The first messenger that gave notice of Lucullus' coming was so far from pleasing Tigranes that he had his head cut off for his pains; and no man daring to bring further information, without

any intelligence at all, Tigranes sat while war was already blazing around him, giving ear only to those who flattered him...".[1]

Another similar instance is found in another ancient text.

In the 'the famous lament of the Spanish Moors Ay de mi Alhama, which tells how King Boabdil received the news of the fall of his city of Alhama. He feels that this loss means the end of his rule. But he will not "let it be true"...."He threw the letters in the fire and killed the messenger"'.[6][1]

The idea of "killing the messenger" is alluded to in several of Shakespeare's dramas as well.

It seems that people don't like to hear bad news, especially if it affects them personally. Sometimes people react violently to truth that challenges their behavior. Such is the case in this passage.

: Amos, the country preacher from Tekoa wasn't the kind of preacher/prophet that made people feel good about themselves.

His message, given to him directly from God, was one condemnation, and pending judgment. Israel had become sinful by engaging in everything from immorality to idolatry. God had had enough and was preparing to judge them. He had given them many, many years to repent and return to holy living. He sent prophet after prophet to warn them, but they ignored them. Now, Amos tells them that judgment is coming-it is irrevocable. It is bad news for sinful Israel and the people don't want to hear it. They were quite comfortable in their sin; they thought that God would bless them no matter what they did.

The last thing they wanted was some uncouth country bumpkin coming into their fine, contemporary, cultured society and telling them they better get right with God or they would soon face His judgment. Amos has pulled no punches, he has delivered the Lord's message, and now the people are ready to "kill the messenger".

Though the events of the book of Amos happened in the 8th century BC, we find God revealing timeless truths throughout the book. In this case, we find the eternal truth that when you speak the Lord's truth, and stand uncompromisingly on His word, when you "tell it like it is", look out! People are going to get angry about it. Someone, somewhere is going to get upset, sometimes violently so. So this passage serves as an encouragement to speak the truth according to Scripture. There is also another thing to glean from the passage:

Nobody likes to be confronted with their sin, but God has a way of doing that very thing and He uses various messengers and messages to do so. So we all need to be reminded, "Don't shoot the messenger when the shoe in on the other foot."

Bearing these things in mind let's divide this passage into two major movements. The first we will call,

The Messenger Accused. Verses 10-13

Verses 10-11

In the preceding passage, Amos showed how God relented in passing judgment on Israel over and over. However, they wouldn't repent. Now, since they didn't measure up to His standards, He would punish them by raising up the Assyrian army to conquer them and take them into exile. This message did not sit well with the Israelites. Nobody likes to be called out and have their sin exposed...but the prophet had no choice. He had to speak the word of the Lord. So Amaziah tries to put a stop to Amos' preaching.

A. The Accuser. Verse 10.

Who is this Amaziah, the priest of Bethel? This is

the only place he is mentioned in Scripture (there was a King Amaziah, but this isn't him). So we have to deduct a few things from the text. First, he was the priest. This indicates he was the head priest or lead priest over several other priests. So he was a big wig.

Secondly, he was a false priest with no authority to serve as one. How do we know this? Because he was the priest of Bethel.

Bethel was NOT the official place of worship-Jerusalem was. King Jeroboam had built an unauthorized temple in Bethel to please the people of the northern kingdom.

It was a place of syncretic worship. They did do a few token sacrifices to God there. They also had a golden calf there and allowed all sorts of debauchery and immorality as they mixed Judaism with pagan worship practices.

As is often the case, Amos, who spoke the truth ,had to deal with an accuser who had political and social clout, but was a "devil in disguise".

We see the character of Amaziah and Jeroboam in 1 Kings 13.33,

After this thing (After erecting the false temple in Bethel) Jeroboam did not turn from his evil way, but made priests for the high places again from among all the people. Any who would, he ordained to be priests of the high places.

B. The Accusation. Verse 11

Well, this was partially true. Amos had prophesied that Israel would go into exile. But he did not say that Jeroboam would personally die by the sword or be killed in battle. This didn't occur. Jeroboam died of natural causes before the exile took place. This was an exaggeration on Amaziah's part meant to infuriate the king. His hope was that the king would execute Amos for sedition or some similar charge.

Amos wasn't involved in some kind of anti-government conspiracy. He was merely preaching what the Lord spoke to him.

You can almost hear the sarcasm and contempt dripping from Amaziah's voice, can't you?

Trust me, when you speak the Lord's word, when you stand up for what's righteous, sooner or later you are going to tick someone off! Your accusers will often operate just like Amaziah. They will take just a little shred of truth and then add a little untruth to it; or take your words out of context, and try to discredit you. It's all an effort to keep you from speaking the truth according to the Scripture.

Ask me how I know!

Eventually, Amaziah confronts Amos. Read verses 12-13. We see here:

C. The Prophet Accosted.

Apparently Amaziah carried some judicial authority granted by the king or at least he thought he did. He orders Amos out of the country! He calls him a "seer" or a prophet. He wasn't using it as a term of respect either. Amaziah grouped Amos with the professional, corrupt, "prophets for hire" that were active in Israel at the time (remember Balaam?).

If you read this in the Hebrew it carries strong language. Amaziah tells Amos to "Get out of Israel, run away, and disappear like a shadow". " Go back home! Your kind doesn't belong here! Go preach in Judah, 'cause that type of preaching just doesn't go over here!

It might have worked in Judah, among the farmers, but here in the city people are better educated, more sophisticated, more "genteel". That hard, direct message offends people of our sensibilities." He tells him to "leave and don't ever come back."

It's amazing to note how Amaziah refers to the place of false worship at Bethel. It is the "king's sanctuary and a temple of the kingdom." This shows just how far Israel had fallen. He didn't even claim that the temple was the "house of God". The implication is that the king set the standards of worship not God! That's just amazing! It also hits closer to home than we care to admit. Whenever unbiblical tradition and manmade, carnal tricks and tactics become the standards for the church-look out! Trouble is coming!

I could give you a hundred personal illustrations of this. But I prefer to turn to the life of our Lord. If anyone suffered false accusations it was He!

In Matthew Chapter 26 we find Jesus before the high priest and his council. He is basically on trial for His life. Listen to this,

Now the chief priests and the whole council were seeking false testimony against Jesus that they might put Him to death, but they found none, though many false witnesses came forward. At last two came forward and said, "This man said, 'I am able to destroy the temple of God, and to rebuild it in three days.'"

And the high priest stood up and said, 'Have you no answer to make? What is it that these men testify against you? " But Jesus remained silent.

And the high priest said to Him, "I adjure you by the living God, tell us if you are the Christ, the Son of God." Jesus said to him, "You have said so. But I tell you, from now on you will see the Son of Man seated at the right hand of Power and coming on the clouds of heaven." Then the priest tore his robes and said, "He has uttered blasphemy. What further witnesses do we need? You have heard His blasphemy."

Can you see how the false accusers twisted His words? How the high priest rejected the truth?

Make no mistake, when you speak the truth, people who are well established in sin will not like it. They will twist your words, or outright lie in order to discredit you. They will also pressure you to be silent by attacking your character and your qualifications. You must not become discouraged when this happens but count yourself blessed.

(Jesus said) *"Blessed are you when others revile you and persecute you and utter all kinds of evil against you falsely on my account. Rejoice and be glad, for your reward is great in heaven, for so they persecuted the prophets who were before you." Matthew 5.11-12*

I also want to remind you to be careful when you are offended because someone told you the truth. Don't twist their words, or try to avert attention by trying to discredit them. The intention is to repent and get right with God, not to shoot the messenger! I'll bet you if you go to any restaurant in town Sunday afternoon, and listen to the conversations around you, will hear this very principle in action.

Some poor preacher somewhere told the truth according to God's Word and the accusations are flying! Think about that if you are ever tempted to do it yourself!

Amos' answer is a "golden moment" in Scripture. The next movement is,

The Messenger's Answer. Verses 14-17

Verses 14-15

Amos says, "I'm no prophet, nor was my daddy a prophet! I'm just a simple farmer who raises sheep and figs. But, the Lord sent me here to preach His word of judgment. He says in essence, "Look, I didn't look up one day and say, 'Hey, I think I'll run over to Israel and tell them that most of them are going to die and the rest are going into exile." It was God who sent him and he was being obedient to the Lord's direction and purpose.

Can I pause and preach for a minute? It's more of a prayer and plea than a sermon. Lord, give us some men; some preachers like Amos today! Give us some men who will obey your call and preach the Word without fear and without watering it down!

Give us some men that will leave the herds, and the fig groves, and the tool shed, and the factory, and the recliner, and the retirement rocking chair, and the classroom and the truck, and the office, and preach the word to a lost and dying world!

Lord, give us some men who aren't afraid to stand against unbiblical practice and doctrine even if it's the way it's always been!

Give us some men who will ignore the physical pain, the emotional toll, the financial burden, the naysayers, the religious people, the ungodly matriarchs and patriarchs of ungodly churches; and fearlessly, even to the point of death- PREACH THE TRUTH! And STAND FOR THE TRUTH. AND LIVE THE TRUTH!

Good God, any preacher these days who has a little backbone, or is more afraid of God than he is of people better watch out! He will get labeled as unloving, or unkind, or not gentle or being a preacher but not a pastor...bah- I hear that every day!

I'd rather stand before God in rags with an Amos spirit, than I would stand before God in Armani with a heart like Balaam-the prophet for hire! (Ok, enough of that!)

Amos not only defends his prophetic ministry but he continues it in the face of this opposition. Look at this:

Verses 16-17

I'll bet he won Amaziah over with that little nugget of prophesy!

He says, "You tell me to shut up, to disappear, to stop this kind of preaching...let me tell you what's coming for you! Your wife will be violated; your children will die in war. All the wealth you have accumulated as a hireling priest for the king will be split up and given to your enemies. You are going to live, but you will be carried off into exile as a slave to the Assyrians. So much for being tactful and sugary, huh?

Now that we have looked at this passage in context; let's ask ourselves: "What can we personally learn from this scenario?

When you are attacked for Christ's sake you must:

1.   Have a realistic view of yourself.   Embrace true humility.

Amos did not thump his chest, or recite his credentials. He gave God all the credit and claimed no authority for himself.

2. Remind your accuser it is the Lord's message you are delivering not your own. Of course, you need to make sure you are speaking and standing on God's Word or the accusations may very well be true!

When people get mad at me for telling them the truth I have a standard answer, "Tell Jesus about it, it's His word."

3. Keep on speaking the truth, proclaiming God's Word and trust the Lord to be with you.

A lot of people give up after just one battle for the truth. Let me tell you can't quit! Ever! You must stand for God and the truth of Scripture until you die or you heard a trumpet and you start ascending!

Jesus told us we would often be put to the test for our faith. He said we may even have to defend our faith in front of the authorities. But he gives us a promise.

(Jesus said) "And when they bring you before the synagogues and the rulers and the authorities, do not be anxious about how you should defend yourself or what you should say, for the Holy Spirit will teach you in that very hour what you ought to say." Luke 12. 11-12

If you are serious about God's Word at some point you will face an accuser, you know their tactics, and you know how to answer. Trust the Lord to give you strength and wisdom. All you need to supply is the courage.

One of the most iconic images of the 20th century was broadcast around the world in on June 5th, 1989. It is the picture of the lone protestor standing in front of a Chinese tank in Tiananmen Square in Beijing. This man was ready to be run over by the tank in order to stand for truth. His friends pulled him to safety but the image lives on to remind us of the power of conviction.

I've often looked at that picture and wondered how frightened and alone that man must have felt.

Oftentimes standing for the truth of God's Word can feel like that: as if you are standing alone in front of a tank and about to be crushed.

But, take heart...God is with you! Even if you give up your life you go on to a grand reward. Most of the time, our standing on the Word isn't that dramatic. But it can get difficult. I pray that through Amos' actions you have found strength to stand when the occasion arises.

That's the message for believers today. But there is also a message for non-believers. God's word says that like Israel in Amos' time, you are doomed unless repent of your sin and turn to Jesus Christ for salvation. Have you? The Word of God says all have sinned. It says that the punishment for that sin is eternal torture in hell. The word also says that God loves you and died on the cross to pay the price for your sin. It says if you call on the name of Jesus you will be saved. You will live forever in glory with Christ someday. What will you do today with this wonderful truth?

[1]http://en.wikipedia.org/wiki   -
Shooting_the_messenger

CHAPTER 17: GOD'S REMARKABLE GRACE AND RESTORATION 9. 11-15

The nation of Israel is once again on the brink of all-out war. Right now there is a massive bombing campaign in Gaza, and artillery exchange with Islamic extremist. It looks like a ground war is imminent. Anyone with a cursory knowledge of end-time prophecy knows that the culmination of many events will be the battle of Armageddon. That's the day when the nations of the world come against the Anti-Christ who will be headquartered in Jerusalem. That is the time when Jesus returns to the earth with the saints to conquer all foes. He will then rule for 1,000 years.

That is coming in the future. However, the events we see unfolding today are not that event. How do I know? Because we are still here! The Bible teaches that Christ calls the church to heaven before the period known as the Tribulation occurs. So relax. The stage is being set, but it isn't time for the final act just yet.

The nation of Israel will always be at war with someone ,and they will always be under threat from surrounding nations. Until the Lord comes, they will never completely occupy the Promised Land.

The Bible does say that all of Israel will be saved. At some point in the end time events, every surviving person in the nation of Israel will confess Jesus Christ as Lord and Savior.

God will never break His promises to His people; even though His chastening, and judgment may be severe. Thus, we come to the final words of Amos' prophecy.

You can imagine that the people of Israel were reeling from Amos' prophetic pronouncements. God was going to judge them for their sin. That judgment was irrevocable! The form of His judgment would be the mighty Assyrian army who would conquer Israel. Kill many of them. Take the rest into slavery. Then they would occupy their land.

By this time, people had probably caught on that disaster was coming and they were no doubt asking, "Is there is any hope?" "Have we sinned beyond all reconciliation?" "Will God be angry with us forever?"

God gives Amos the answers to this question, and it is a gracious, "Yes!"

The eternal instruction we take from this passage is this: God loves you and even though there are periods of discipline, even punishment for your actions, you can always come back to Him. That would be good enough, but God is much more gracious than we can imagine. When you come back to Him; He not only forgives you ,but He restores you, blesses you, and re-affirms you as His everlasting child.

The previous statement constitutes the three major truths we want to focus on in this chapter. The first truth is:

God's Promise of Restoration. Verses 11-12

Verse 11

In that day" refers to the "Day of the Lord". This term is used throughout Scripture signifying many different aspects of the Lord's dealings with Israel. What it refers to here is the time when the long exile will be over, and Israel will return to her homeland.

Notice how Amos describes God's restoration of His beloved nation. He will:

1. Raise up the "booth" of David, repair its breaches, raise up its ruins and rebuild it as in the days of old. (And you thought that alliterating sermon points was a modern invention!)

He refers to the nation of Israel as a "booth" or a "tent". This stresses the severity of the destruction Israel experienced at the hands of the Assyrians.

The nation was a great fortress, but now it is just a little, dilapidated tent. But-God is going to raise it up-give it new life-make it glorious, and strong once again.

The walls of an ancient city were thick and served to protect the city from siege. When the walls of a city were breached, the invader poured into the city and could not be stopped. Amos says the broken walls would be repaired; the cities of Israel would be protected once again.

The homes and buildings that were devastated by war will be rebuilt. The nation that looked like it would fade into the annuals of history will once again be recognized as God's unique people.

Verse 12

Amos now foresees far into the future to the earthly ministry, and eventual earthly reign of Christ. Edom is representative of all mankind. This speaks to the inclusion of the Gentiles in the Messiah's salvation. It also foretells of Christ's return, when He will rule over the nations from Israel, specifically from Jerusalem.

God not only excels at creation, but He is also a Master of restoration!

I don't think we fully appreciate just how terrible the Fall of Man truly was. In the beginning, the world was perfect, everything worked perfectly.

There was no sickness or death, crops grew, animals were friendly, God and mankind had unbroken fellowship. Yet, Adam and Eve, when tempted by Satan, fell, and in them humanity fell, and the world has been messed up ever since.

Only through the sacrifice of Jesus Christ was a way made possible to escape the curse of the Fall. However, don't you find it remarkable that God made it possible to be restored to fellowship and peace with Him?

It's amazing that God didn't wipe Adam and Eve off the face of the earth and call humanity a botched experiment. He allowed them to live. He continued to bless them with children and their children with children...until here we are today; with a hope and promise of full restoration in Jesus Christ. Amazing!

While this particular promise was given (partially in the return from exile, fully in the redemptive work of Christ) to ancient Israel, there is an eternal promise found in it for all believers. It is this: *No matter how severely God chastens His people, no matter how devastated they may become; once repentance is expressed; He will graciously return His favor and blessing. The ultimate expression of this will be the believer's eternal life of blessing and rewards in heaven.*

(Jesus said) "The Spirit of the Lord is upon me, because He has anointed me to proclaim good news to the poor. He has sent me to proclaim liberty to the captives and recovering of sight to the blind, to set at liberty those who are oppressed, to proclaim the year of the Lord's favor." Luke 4. 18-19

God goes beyond mere restoration, To those who turn to Him in faith and repentance, it just gets better and better. Next consider,

God's Promise of Abundance. Verses 13-14

Verse 13

The Lord declares, He decrees, He makes a holy proclamation, that abundance is coming to Israel. The imagery is spectacular. God says that there will be so much abundance that the harvesters will still be harvesting while the planters sow seed for the next season!

And the wine!

In Amos' day, wine was used as currency. To have a large quantity of wine meant a great deal of wealth. It meant the Lord had blessed with a great harvest and the fermentation process had gone well. The mountain side will drip with wine; it will collect in the foothills and flow through the ravines like streams. This is not a wino's wish come true, and should not be taken literally. It is, however, strong metaphorical language describing superabundance.

Verse 14

Here is another promise that God is going to restore Israel's fortunes and status. One of God's judgments was that Israel's homes and lands would be occupied by the invaders. Yet, here we see Israel gets it all back- and then some.

This is God in His element.

Even though His people can act very badly, when they finally come to their senses, He not only restores them, but blesses them beyond all imagination.

Jesus' parable of the prodigal son is the perfect illustration of this truth. Take a minute and read Luke 16.

11-24.

Seriously, do it. It's a great story!

Did you read it? Did it make your heart soar? Told ya'!

The son finally came to his senses and went home and asked for forgiveness. The father not only forgave him and restored him to the family, but he gave him over and above what he expected. He was given full status in the family. He was given new clothes and new shoes. They killed the best beef, and a great party was held to celebrate his return.

God will do the same for you if you will just turn to Him in faith and repentance.

Once again we must note that the final consummation of this truth will come when Christ returns. However, we see the "spirit" of this promise fulfilled in all aspects of salvation. God blesses us more than we can imagine. From fruit of the spirit, to actual material blessings; God pours great quantities of high quality benefits upon His people. This is made even more remarkable in that He does this even when we have sinned and rebelled.

Paul wrote to the church at Corinth,

"But as it is written, "What eye has not seen, nor ear heard, nor the heart of man imagined, what God has prepared for those who love Him"-

I Corinthians 2.9 Cf. Isaiah 64.4)

So God promises restoration, and He promises abundance. Let's look at one final promise before we leave the book of Amos. It is,

God's Promise of Security.

Verse 15

This is yet to be fulfilled. Israel does occupy a great deal of the Promised Land, but not 100% of it. There were also several periods of exile after the Assyrian exiles were allowed to return. So this is interpreted as referring to the eternal security that Christ promises to all those who believe. The promise of salvation, the hope we cling to in difficult times is that nothing can "separate us from the love of Christ".

Notice the language used here: *I will plant them on their land...they will never be uprooted again, I gave the land thus says the Lord!*

There is nothing in this world that is permanent, even the earth will pass away; but God promises eternal security to all true believers. A new heaven and a new earth and a New Jerusalem are coming-He has guaranteed it. They will not be subject to decay, or erosion or war or famine or drought.

God's people will never grow old, or be sick or die, or sin again. How's that for security?

This promise was partially fulfilled in the exiles' return to Northern Kingdom during the time of Ezra and Nehemiah.

The ultimate fulfillment (of this promise of security) will come during the reign of Christ when "all Israel will be saved" (Romans 11).

This promise finds universal application to all believers, in that God will ultimately reward them with a permanent dwelling, and everlasting life in glory.

John the Revelator tells us:

And I heard a loud voice from the throne saying, "Behold, the dwelling place of God is with man. He will dwell with them, and they will be His people, and God himself will be with them as their God. He will wipe every tear from their eyes, and death shall be no more, neither shall there be mourning, nor crying, nor pain anymore, for the former things have passed away."

Revelation 21. 3-4

So we conclude our journey with Amos. We see that no matter what happens in this life, there is a happy ending for all those who love the Lord.

I want to ask you some important questions:

"Where do you stand with God?"

"Have you been born again?"

" Have you confessed your sin before God, asked His forgiveness and repented?"

" Have you received the grace that God has in abundance for you?"

"Christian, are you going through a season of chastening?"

"Does it feel like your life is in pieces?"

" Does it feel like you have gone too far and there is no turning back."

Let me conclude this book with some lyrics from an old song we used to sing back during the Jesus movement. It's called, *Pick Up the Broken Pieces.* The song was written by Ruby Kitchen and James Martin. Let these lines speak to your heart:

Have you failed in life's battle to accomplish your plans?

Is your heart heavy laden?

Do you fear the lord's command?

Do you feel that no one loves you,

and there's no use to try?

Just bring your cares to Jesus, your soul

He'll satisfy.

Pick up the broken pieces,

and bring them to the Lord.

Pick up the broken pieces, trust in his holy word.

He will put them back together,

and make your life complete.

Just place the broken pieces at the savior's feet.

You may feel that there's no hope,

broken hearts just cannot mend.

Tho' you're torn in many pieces,

Christ can make you whole again.

Storms of doubt blow all directions,

but do not be afraid.

God can make all corrections.

He made a body out of clay.

BIBLIOGRAPHY

Comfort, Philip W. General Editor. *Tyndale Cornertone Biblical Commentary* (Carol Stream, Ill. Tyndale House Publishers. Inc.: 2008)

Longman Tremper, III & Garland, David E. General EdiGtors. *The Expositor's Bible Commentary* (Grand Rapids, MI. Zondervan: 2008)

Mcgee, Veron *Thru-the Bible Commentary Series, Zephaniah, and Haggai*: (Nashville, TN. Thomas Nelson: 1991)

Mohler, Albert R. Jr. *He is Not Silent*: *Preaching in a Postmodern* : (Chicago, Ill. Moody: 2008)

Swindoll, Charles R. **Tale of the Tardy Ox-Cart** (Nashville, TN. Word Publishing: 1998)

PS:

People who know me will tell you that I've been promising this book for over two years now. To them, I apologize. You all know what chaos my life has been since June of 2020. I pray reading this book was worth the wait.

For those of you who don't know me, allow me this opportunity to thank you for granting me a bit of your time. I have four other books that may be of interest to you. Here are the links,

https://www.amazon.com/When-Righteous-Suffer-Messages-Job-ebook/dp/B0815XC33G/ref=sr_1_1?
crid=SML7D4QGXLPQ&keywords=thomas+leach
+job&qid=1646590862&sprefix=thomas+leach+job%2Caps
%2C81&sr=8-1

https://www.amazon.com/Consider-Your-Ways-Messages-Haggai-ebook/dp/B07YM3PQPM/ref=sr_1_1?
crid=DSWZEFKZSEIN&keywords=thomas+leach
+haggai&qid=1646590959&sprefix=thomas+leach+haggai
%2Caps%2C78&sr=8-1

https://www.amazon.com/Dont-Hypocrite-Authentic-Christianity-Expository-ebook/dp/B07YCT98T9/ref=sr_1_1?
crid=2EPP1XPXWE9YJ&keywords=thomas+leach
+hypocrite&qid=1646590999&sprefix=thomas+leach
+hypocrite%2Caps%2C78&sr=8-1

https://www.amazon.com/When-Misfits-Rise-Judges-11-ebook/dp/B09NMTS2KF/ref=sr_1_1?
crid=AG5DRGDG9ZRJ&keywords=thomas+leach+misfits&qid=1646591038&sprefix=thomas+leach+misfits%2Caps%2C83&sr=8-1